SPRINT KARTING

A COMPLETE BEGINNER'S GUIDE

Jean L. Genibrel

Genibrel
PUBLICATIONS

© 2000 Genibrel Publications

5318 East Second Street, PMB 747
Long Beach, California 90803
(562) 434-3301

ISBN 0-9669120-1-2
10 9 8 7 6 5 4 3 2 1

TABLE OF CONTENTS

ABOUT THE AUTHOR

Born in France and raised in Canada, Jean Genibrel has made the U.S. his home since 1964. The author began his racing career in 1968 with an Austin Healy Sprite in local events. Later, Genibrel drove a Mini-Stock for a local team and received his first SCCA license in 1969 racing a Gordini. Genibrel worked for several professional teams, notably Dan Gurney's All American Racers in the Bobby Unser and Jerry Grant days, Dick Guldstrand Enterprises, and many other SCCA, IMSA and Trans Am Teams. Jean built and raced several record setting project cars and engines for various teams and publications, ranging from Stock Cars, to karts and SCCA sedans.

Jean Genibrel has five books to his credit and collaborated on three more as an editor for "Steve Smith Autosports Publications". Genibrel began racing karts in 1982 at Ascot Park in Gardena, California, and he has raced karts on most of the tracks in the southwest. Jean was president of the San Fernando Valley Kart Club in the mid '80s.

Jean Genibrel is best known for his karting publications, "The Beginners' Complete Karting Guide", "Racing the Yamaha KT100S", and "4-Cycle Karting Technology" which he co-authored. Since 1982 Jean has been contributing editor to National Kart News, Karttech, Circle Track, Short Track Racing, Sport Compact Car, Popular Hot Rodding, Stock Car Racing, and Bracket Racing USA. Genibrel was the tech editor of Rod Action & Street Machines and most recently created, produced and edited Kart Racer magazine. In May 1998, Jean was the first journalist awarded for a karting story. Genibrel received the STP award at the 1998 Indy 500 banquet of the American Auto Racing Writers & Broadcasters Association.

Genibrel Publications recently published "Karting! A Complete Introduction". The tome assists prospective karters in entering the sport economically and easily. The author/publisher plans to produce a complete library of karting books, including the next in the series, which will cover the Yamaha KT100S kart-racing engine. He will translate some of the books into French.

ACKNOWLEDGMENTS

- Bill Barros, Empire Karts
- Cameron Evans, Popular Hot Rodding
- Colin Iwasa, Yamaha Motor Corporation USA
- Dave Klaus, Briggs & Stratton
- Doug Fleming, Pitts Performance
- E.C. Birt, EC Tillotson USA.
- E.J. Korecky, E.J.'s Creations
- Fred Gerrior, Yellow Fin Racing
- George Sieracki, CG Racing
- Jean Marchioni, JM Racing
- Kerry Rauch, TRICK Fuel
- Kurt Burris, Burris Racing
- Mark Adelizzi, Flat Out Group
- Mark Homchick, Kawasaki MotorsUSA
- National Kart News Magazine
- Nate Shelton, Tom Cates, Brian Cornelius, K&N Engineering Inc.
- Rich Hearn, Hearn Competition Karting
- Rob Liptle Honda Motors USA
- Sean and Greg Buur, Go Racing Magazine
- Sven Pruett
- Tim Kerrigan, Dave Granquist, RedLine Oil Co.
- Todd Thelen US820
- And Dan Moran, Larry LaCost Jr., Dave Romero, Pete Muller, Mark Weaverling, and Bill Gates

SPECIAL THANKS TO

- Go Racing Magazine for the main cover photo and others throughout this book, and for their fine effort in promoting karting.
- Hearn Competition Karting for their help in making this book possible.
- J.M. Racing for allowing the author to spend too much time at the shop when doing photography.
- J.P. Mechin who permitted the reproduction of drawings from his book: "Chassis De Kart".
- Pete Muller for "The Karting Web Site" on the internet at www.muller.net.

DEDICATION
This book is dedicated to the memory of Greg Moore and Gonzalo Rodriguez.

DESIGN/LAYOUT
Kimmie Sirimitr

PHOTO CREDITS
Mark Adelizzi, John Bigelow, Sean Buur, Scott Cramer, Rich Hlaves, E.J. Korecky, Tyler Marshall, Jody Mercer, Brian Van Horn, Speed Graphics, Dick Sander, Jean Genibrel.

INTRODUCTION

When I wrote my first karting books in 1984, not much information was available on the sport of karting. Racers would learn from one another and from personal experience. Since then many things have changed, but as they say: "The more things change the more they stay the same!" The karts have grown quite sophisticated and the engines are turning considerably more speed and producing more power than they did just a decade ago. Focus on the basics endures.

Much like the masons of antiquity, today's masons still use the square, the level and the plumb as their basic tools, and those tools still establish the basic principles of their trade; racers must learn to focus on their basic tools and principles. Focusing on the basics is the recurring theme of this book; this made choosing a precise title for this book a difficult task.

I feared the beginners would look at the book as a tool for the experienced karters. On the other hand, I considered the experienced karters would shy away from it for fear of relegating themselves to the level of beginners. The truth is that racers of all levels are always beginners; there is always something to learn (or unlearn). Each day. Each turn. Each race. Racers often blame their engine, tires or small budget for their poor performance. Instead, they should focus on their mental, emotional and physical skills as they relate to their driving. Then, once the basics are mastered, they can fine-tune their mechanical skills. In racing, the most important part to tune is the one which sets atop the driver's shoulders; for the beginner and just as importantly for the experienced karter. Professional teams work the basics on a regular basis and those who do it more than the others do seem to win more games or races, and they accumulate more championships.

Focus is most important for the new racer. "Knowledge is more powerful than power." Nevertheless, knowing what to learn and what not to listen to is key. In the book you are holding, I impart the experience I gained in my near two decades in all phases of karting and the three decades in motorsports in general to help the newcomer (and not so new comer) separate the real basics from the fallacies, the truths from the pipedreams and the important from the irrelevant. Most significantly, the book will teach you which basics to focus on.

Focusing on the basics will allow the new sprinter to learn the "tricks" (there are no such things, but let your competitors think so) while he is learning how to drive. In any sport, the players always rely on the basics. The talent and experience of course play a role, but the beginning karter does not know if he has the talent until he has spent some time racing and gained some experience. Most driving experts will tell you that driving is a learned art, something that needs to be practiced as well as taught. Unfortunately, most new racers think that karting technology is so simple, and the (experienced) drivers make it look so easy, that they assume the driver must not have much to do in the equation. Others think they just know they are as good a driver as the other guy (it's a guy thing); so they look for the little "tricks of the trade", which typically do not exist. In fact, the National Champions interviewed in writing this book and other pieces I worked on maintain, with just cause, that it is the basics applied with focused driving and preparation that win races. Our books can teach you the basics; you focus.

Godspeed

Jean L. Genibrel (signature)

Jean L. Genibrel

Chapter 1
GOING KARTING
Focus and Perspective

Many a professional race driver had his start in karting: Scott Pruett, Richie Hearn, Alex Barron, Brian Herta, Cruz, Tony and Frank Pedregon, and of course Canadian World Formula One Champion Jacques Villeneuve are all ex-champion karters. America had a World Karting Champion in NASCAR driver Lake Speed. Most of the Formula 1 and CART drivers had at least some karting experience. In Europe, and most developed countries of the world, except America, (what is wrong with this picture?) professional teams and automobile manufacturers sponsor karters and place them in their "Ladder System" which leads to a complete "Campus" for race drivers and a potential Formula One or CART ride.

Karting is the best way to get into racing. As Ayrton Senna said: "Karting is the purest form of motorsport." And rightly so. With its simple chassis, single cylinder engine, lack of gearbox (at least in the beginner classes) and basic chain drive, karting has proven to yield the most bang for the buck over any other form of motorsport. The early age at which karting can be entered allows a youngster to amass more driving experience by the time he is 18 than many professional drivers had at their peak a few decades ago.

Karting Around The World

There are over one hundred thousand karters in the U.S. and Canada, and nearly one million around the globe. Following its inception on the parking lots of Pasadena, California, in 1956, the sport spread throughout the world in less than two years. Karting is now only practiced on purpose-built tracks designed with "safety first" in mind. It is illegal to drive karts on private properties, parking lots, alleys and public streets. This practice is very dangerous. "Playing around" with a kart on an unapproved location or while not wearing the proper equipment causes more injuries than racing on proper tracks.

Clubs, national and international organizations sanction most of kart racing. The International Kart Federation (IKF), Karters

Alex Barron started racing karts at the age of 9. Driving for JM Racing, Alex made a name for himself winning a multitude of races and championships and he is on his way to a promising Indy Car career. Alex believes that his success is based on focus, persistence and perspective.

Karts have changed a lot since Art Ingels built the first "go-kart" in 1956. This Ingels "go-kart", the oldest in the world, is still in the possession of his widow Ruth. The shirt Art wore to race lays on the seat.

of America Racing Triad (KART) and the World Karting Association (WKA) regulate karting in the U.S. The local clubs in the U.S. run under the umbrella of at least one of those organizations, or at least they follow the associations' rules and safety regulations. Many clubs race under the insurance provided by the associations. As a driver or crewmember you will be required to pay for a pit pass, which includes the insurance, each time you enter a race sanctioned by your organization. Canadian karting is governed by the ASN Canada, a division of the Federation Internationale de l' Automobile (FIA). In all other countries, karting is regulated by the Federation Mondiale de Karting/Federation Internationale de l' Automobile (FMK/FIA), based in France and Switzerland respectively.

These magazines are the official publications of the American and Canadian karting organisations. Each year the organisations produce a rulebook for their members.

In Europe, karting receives the utmost respect from the public, and the drivers are revered as the embodiment of the consum-

mate racer. In Italy, France or Britain, a driver's chances of progressing into F3, and later Formula 1, are almost nil if he has not participated in karting. A national and certainly a world karting championship almost guarantee a driver a seat with a professional team in a world class series.

Sprint Karting

Recognized as the epitome of kart racing, sprint is the most common around the world, and it is what most people think of when the word "karting" is mentioned. Sprint karting is practiced on short tracks, generally one quarter to three quarter miles in length. The tracks are asphalt or concrete. A typical sprint race consists of 2 or 3 practice and tuning sessions, 2 or 3 heats of 5 to 10 minutes, and then the event is capped by a main event.

American sprint karting offers many possibilities. There are several types of engines to choose from and a multitude of classes. These lads are racing US820 engines.

Sprint karting, much like the other divisions of the sport, is divided into classes based on age, engine type (two- and four-cycle), brand, modifications, and individual specifications such as muffler, or type or size of carburetor, and a weight minimum of the driver and kart combination. In addition, some clubs run "local options" such as a tire rule (which consists of a hard compound to prevent rapid wear). For example, a class could be for drivers over 18 years of age, running a Yamaha KT100S, under "Stock rules", with a "Can" muffler and spec tires, at 350 pounds minimum. All sprint classes run on slick tires, except in the rain.

In the mid 1970s, Americans started yet another form of karting: "shifters". Some wisenheimer decided to strap on an engine off a motocross bike to a kart chassis; a new form of motorsport was born. Shifters are raced primarily in the U.S. and Canada.

Sprint karting is the epitome of kart racing. It is the most prevalent form of karting around the world. Only in the U.S. are karts raced on the dirt and on long sports car courses.

Other Forms of American Karting

Kart oval track racing is very important in the U.S. Speedway (dirt oval) is most prevalent east of the Rockies, with the South and the Midwest the hotbeds of this form of racing. Dirt tracks are composed of clay, sand, or cinder. Most dirt ovals are 1/10th to 1/4 mile in length, although some clubs may run on 1/2 mile tracks. The surfaces are watered and groomed before the events begin in order to reduce the dust and to provide adequate traction. Dirt track racers use grooved or treaded tires to allow the treads to sink into the track to provide traction, although many tracks are going to the "slicks only" rule.

"Enduro" as the name implies, is a test of endurance for the driver as well as the kart and engine. These events are run on long sports-car road courses such as Mosport, Sears Point Raceway, Road America, Watkins Glen, Charlotte and Daytona. An enduro can last 45 minutes to an hour. The speeds attained can reach 120 to 125 miles-per-hour due to the length of the tracks raced on and the laid down position of the drivers, which reduces aerodynamic drag. The low, long, sleek shape and appearance and its characteristic butterfly steering wheel easily identify an enduro kart.

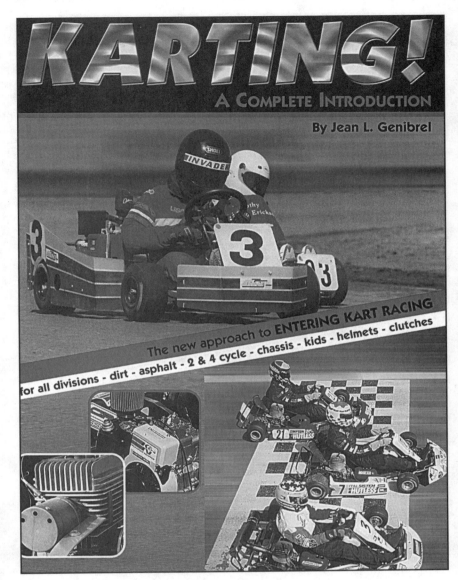

KARTING!
A COMPLETE INTRODUCTION
By Jean L. Genibrel

The new approach to ENTERING KART RACING

for all divisions - dirt - asphalt - 2 & 4 cycle - chassis - kids - helmets - clutches

In the U.S., karts also race on long sports car courses. The sprinters run on these tracks are sometimes referred to as road racers. Others are "lay-downs" which are easily recognized by their long, sleek shapes.

"Road Racing" is the name used for the sprint karts that run on the larger road courses. The shifters form a large contingent in road racing. Most clubs and organizations have classes for the shifters. "Shifter Kart Illustrated" magazine specializes in shifter kart racing.

Typically, the power plants are modified motocross engines. The major suppliers of engines to the shifter classes are: Honda, Kawasaki, TM, Vortex and Yamaha, with Rotax making a presence in the 250cc ranks. Classes are available for 60, 80, 125 and 250 cubic centimeters. Older, well-experienced and financed drivers primarily race the 125 and 250 classes. The smaller

Genibrel Publications produces a complete line of karting books. "Karting! A Complete Introduction" is a great help in getting newcomers into the sport.

Dirt track karting is typically American. The karts are usually "offset" to carry more weight on the left and the tires are grooved to provide traction in the mud. "Speedway" as it is often called is mostly practiced in the South and Midwest.

Karting boasts of the most friendly participants. New-comers are never left in the cold and someone more experienced is always willing to lend a hand or give advice.

to 20 times less than a small open-wheel, road race sedan or drag car.

A novice season of sprint karting may include the cost of a piston and 2 or 3 sets of rings, a couple of sets of tires in a tire rule class, and a few gallons of gasoline. Even the karts which run on methanol burn less than a gallon of fuel per race. Oil used in a season is less than a dozen quarts, compared to a case per race with a full size car.

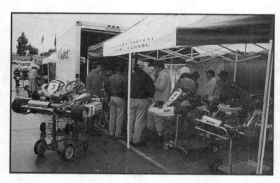

Karting schools such as KRC seen in this photo, are an excellent way of getting into karting. Some of these schools offer "arrive and drive" programs where the driver does not have to invest in the equipment.

displacement classes are open to drivers of 10 years of age and up. Chapter 13 of this book covers the shifters in detail.

Practice Karting and Arrive and Drive

Many also enjoy karting as a form of non-competitive recreation. "Practice Karters" enjoy this form of racing without entering races. They simply go to a track on a non-race day, pay a small entry fee, sign the insurance waiver and they practice all day. There is always someone at the track to chat with and form new friendships. Many drivers move up to racing with a club when they feel more confident about their driving abilities and tuning skills.

Some shops, schools and tracks offer "Arrive and Drive" programs. The driver effectively rents the kart and sometimes a mechanic for the duration of the event. The driver can choose the events he wants to run, or some organizations have events in which the driver can participate. If after a season of Arrive and Drive he decides not to continue in karting, he simply walks away. On the other hand, a karter who has invested in the equipment would have to sell it if he chooses to abandon the sport.

Costs

Karting is the least expensive form of motorsport, bar none. A sprinter can purchase a kart and competitive engine for 10

The best way to keep costs low the first season is to enter a well represented class, one which allows few modifications, and one which enforces a tire rule.

Venues

There are over 420 locations in the U.S. where karts can be raced. This includes some of the superspeedways, which incorporate sports-car road courses in the infield where karts can race, like Charlotte Motor Speedway where the World Championship tour stops each year in the fall. Other kart tracks are part of the infield of small ovals.

Of those 420 venues about half are dirt or

You can invest in a truck and trailer when you get serious about your racing. In the beginning however, perspective and learning should be the focus of the novice.

International karting is growing rapidly in North America. The European drivers visit the American continent twice a year. This gives many American and Canadian karters international experience.

asphalt ovals, and the other half are sprint tracks. Many kart tracks maintain their own club, and some clubs maintain their own track. There are 175 kart clubs in the U.S., and 23 clubs and 27 tracks in Canada.

Engines

Kart racing in the U.S. and Canada offers racing in two and four-cycle. The most dominant engines in Canada are the Yamaha KT100S two-cycle and the Honda GX four-cycle. In the U.S., the Yamaha is the main two-cycle with the Horstman HPV appealing at an increasing rate to novices and advanced karters alike. The US820 makes a powerful presence in some parts of the U.S. primarily on the East Coast and Midwest.

The Briggs & Stratton four-stroke leads the way in the States in four-cycle racing. Tecumseh and Honda are making rapid growth in many areas.

New karters should choose an engine primarily based on the availability of tracks in their area and clubs that allow the engine.

American and Canadian karting use primarily two cycle engines. In this photo, several Yamahas await rebuilding at Emmick Enterprises in Sacramento, California. Note the different types of exhaust systems.

Parts availability and local engine builders are also important considerations. By remaining within the "stock" classes, the novice can keep his costs low. The simplicity of tuning and maintenance will allow the novice to concentrate on his driving and learning process. The book "Karting! A Complete Introduction" from this publisher covers the kart engines used in the U.S. and Canada in detail.

Classes

American and Canadian karting classes are based on the engine type (two- or four-cycle) or brand being used, engine modifications, driver's age and overall weight of the kart and driver package. Most classes are composed of a particular engine such as the Yamaha KT100S or the Briggs & Stratton.

The classes are then broken-down by the degree of engine modifications, and the minimum weight of the kart and driver combination. The Junior classes start at 5 and progress to 16. Classes are also formed around some exhaust systems to limit the engine speed, to facilitate tuning, and to

The "can" has been a great boost to American karting. These exhaust systems limit engine noise and speed, which greatly reduce the rebuild and maintenance intervals. These are the brainchildren of RLV of Santa Maria, California.

Some clubs mark the "spec tires." This is a great way of keeping costs down. These tires are generally of a harder compound and they last longer than the softer ones. Note the tech inspector in the background checking if you followed the safety guidelines given in this book.

Keeping things in perspective is probably the best advice anyone can give to a new karter. "Rome was not built in a day" and neither was any professional sport career. Learning the basics of driving are the foundation of any race driver's future.

reduce costs. So a class could be built around the Tecumseh four-cycle, prepared to stock rules, for drivers over 16 years of age and at a minimum weight of 350 pounds combined weight of driver and kart, running on methanol and with an open tire rule. There are classes for drivers over 40.

Some classes require "spec tires." These classes are more economical as the tires last longer than the "open tire" classes.

Decisions

The most important considerations a new karter should take are his age, financial and marital statuses, the amount of time he has available to invest in working on the equipment and traveling. The amount of racing experience he possesses and his ultimate goals in motorsports play a role in deciding what form of karting a newcomer should enter, or which type of engine he should race. An experienced motorcycle racer, or full size race car driver may be comfortable with a "shifter". On the other hand, a middle-aged driver would probably be more comfortable in a more sedate class with a stock engine, restricted exhaust and tire rule. If the driver is a youngster who has (with his parents' support) an eye on professional motorsports as a career, the approach to entering the sport may be more costly and time-consuming than for an older driver who is just looking for a hobby requiring some mechanical abilities in a competitive motorsport.

Goal Setting

Experienced karters are encouraged to read this book, as it is always a good idea to return to basics, especially after a year or

two of racing. The reason is that some drivers may have picked up bad habits and a little review might be worth a few tenths or a position or two. Small things that may have been forgotten or never learned in the first place can make a difference.

Whether a totally "green" driver, or a more experienced karter is reading this text, goal setting is very important and should be part of the planning process. The first advice that can be given is to set realistic goals. For example, do not set a goal of winning your race the first (or second) time out. For the beginning sprinter, a more realistic goal would be to read this book and take notes, and set up the kart based on the guidelines outlined herein.

The next realistic goal may be to attend a

These young men are proud of their WKA winnings. Setting small short term goals lead to meeting larger long term goals. Perseverance and hard work may take them to Indy or Daytona some day. Why not? Most Indy car and Formula 1 drivers started racing karts.

day of practice before entering a race. At the practice, then set goals which will help you achieve other goals, for instance: understanding the instruments, learning how to adjust the carburetor, feeling comfortable in the turns, etc. Setting goals with numbers on them, such as "turn a lap time of 64 seconds or better" is foolish in the beginning. Another example of this would be to set a goal of "finish in the top 5." More realistic goals would be to just understand what is going on and develop a "feel" for the kart and being able to place it where it belongs on the track, such as on the apexes and hitting the braking points, turn ins and acceleration points accurately. Most importantly, remember to always focus and keep things in perspective.

Chapter 2
SAFETY
The Most Dangerous Part of a Kart is Often the Nut Behind the Wheel

Being safe in karting extends farther than when the driver is racing on the track. Safety starts at home when working on the kart, while towing to the track, at the track in the pits and while racing. Even a minor injury can prevent a karter from going to work on Monday morning.

At Home

Many precautions should be taken when working on machinery, engines and with fuels. Karters handle potentially dangerous materials and products on a daily basis. Fuel can burn. Brake fluid and oil are very slippery. Exhaust systems can get extremely hot. Electrical cords can short and cause a fire or shock. Batteries if not properly charged can explode and spew acid over a wide area. Drill bits, saw blades and razor blades can cut. Eye protection should be worn whenever handling fuel, acid or brake fluid and when machining, drilling, grinding or welding.

Check electrical circuit breakers to ensure they can withstand the loads that will be placed on them. Store fuel in steel cans and in a steel cabinet. Keep floors free of trash,

Even a minor injury can keep you from racing or going to work on Monday morning. Wear the appropriate safety equipment when working on the kart, on machinery or when handling chemicals such as fuel. Hearing loss is a common problem among older engine builders and racers who did not heed simple safety precautions.

Ensure that your electrical outlets and cords are up to the job. For welders and large machines like lathes, a 220-volt circuit is necessary. Hire a qualified electrician to install or check your circuits.

boxes and slippery materials to prevent slips and falls.

When lifting heavy objects (a kart for example), get some help and lift with the back straight.

Towing

Many racers have found that towing and driving long distances on the open highway can be more hazardous than racing. Lack of sleep, too much sun and frayed nerves have caused racers more accidents off the track than on the track.

Racers, being what they are, have been known to leave their work on Friday night and arrive at the race track the next morning just in time for the first practice. Not only is this dangerous on the way to the track, but by the time he leaves the track on Sunday and drives back home all night, the driver will be so far behind on his sleep that he will be endangering himself, his passengers and other motorists. Not to mention the treatment his co-workers will have to endure on Monday morning.

Many a racer has been injured, or worse, when towing, even for short hauls. Make sure your towing equipment is safe and legal. Note safety chains, hefty hitch and wiring job on this truck and trailer.

Each state and province has its own towing laws. The law of common sense should prevail everywhere. The most common dangerous practice in towing is overloading of a tow truck or trailer. An overloaded trailer or tow vehicle will tend to fish-tail and its brakes can overheat on down hills. Stopping distances will increase with the weight carried, and the tires can overheat and blow if overloaded.

Trailers should never exceed the weight of the tow vehicle. This would cause the "tail that wagged the dog" syndrome. Furthermore, the trailer and tow truck package will probably exceed the rated weight carrying capacity of the brakes. Trailer brakes are always a good idea and you should not be afraid of over-braking a trailer.

In The Pits

The most common hazards in the pits include burns, abrasions, cuts, sunburns and strained backs. Granted, most of those injuries are minor and certainly not life threatening, but they certainly can influence the quality of life.

Gloves are necessary when working around hot exhausts and clutches. Gloves can also prevent cuts, scrapes and punctures from safety wire and tie strap ends.

Abrasions and broken bones can occur when someone trips over parts or equipment, which have been left in the open.

Cut off the nylon tie straps flush. The ends can cut deep into the skin if left exposed. Bend back the end of safety wire and cotter pins onto themselves. An exposed end can cause nasty punctures and cuts.

A well organised, properly lit and clean trailer will be safe and will make things easy to find. Secure pressurised air tanks to the walls of the trailer and install a safety cap over the valve during transportation.

Toolboxes, starters, wheels and tires, drills and air tanks are common culprits.

Hold a quick pit meeting before the truck is unloaded and remind your crew to pick-up after themselves and to replace the equipment as soon as they are done using it. Not only is this a good safety measure to endorse, but it will make things easier to find and prevent belongings from being left behind after the event.

Fire Prevention

Fire is the most devastating danger. It is the one form of accident which can completely destroy vehicles, equipment, karts and lives in a few seconds. There are a few steps which can be taken to prevent fires in the first place.

Keep fuel in metal containers. A plastic jug is prone to static electricity, which can cause sparks and start a fire. In a fire, the plastic will melt in seconds, literally adding fuel to the fire.

Keep welding equipment in proper operating condition. Have a welding shop inspect the valves, torches and hoses. They will probably be glad to do this free of charge. Note the fire extinguisher mounted near where fire is likely to start.

- Keep fuels in sealed metal containers
- Use a fuel container with a "dead-man's valve"
- Keep several fire extinguishers at home and at the track
- Do not keep damp rags around. Wash them out in hot water and hang them to dry
- Do not refuel your kart when the engine is hot or running
- Do not smoke or use open flames around fuels
- Repair fuel leaks immediately
- Make sure the caps are securely tightened on the gas tank and your fuel containers
- Use common sense

On The Track

The best method of preventing an accident is to not get into one in the first place. The better drivers seldom get into altercations because they are generally near the front where there are fewer karts to get in the way if one spins, and they have better control of the kart from experience and practice. Unfortunately, the newer karters generally start races farther back with other inexperienced drivers.

"Track rage" should never happen! If you feel too uptight to drive, don't drive!

Keep the back straight when picking up heavy objects as demonstrated by the handsome fellow on the left; knees bent, arms straight, back straight, shoulders back of the knees. The fellow on the right is leaning over too much and should be bending the knees more. Push up with the legs and keep the stand next to the kart. PS: Let the young guys pickup the heavy end of the kart.

The pits can get chaotic at times. Keep things organized and clean of spills and trash. Sunshades will help protect against sunburns and dehydration, and outside of California, against rain.

Remember that the most dangerous part of a race kart is usually the nut behind the wheel. At times, drivers "take things personal" and they drive over their abilities to make up for lost positions or to get even with another driver who may not have had anything to do with what the first driver was upset about in the first place. Controlling emotions and one's temper is part of the learning curve.

Concentration and control come after much practice and training. Try to learn from being passed or even bumped. If a driver behind you is getting impatient, let him pass. With seat time you will learn how to stay out of harm's way and to drive your own race without worrying about the other guys. Even the best karters have been through this process and nobody is different.

Conditioning

Being fit will not only help in preventing accidents because it will prevent the driver from becoming tired, but it will help in reducing the severity of injuries if an accident does occur. A simple exercise program at the local gym, daily swims or walks can go a long way in dropping those extra pounds and sharpening the reflexes. Using a speed bag is another way to work-up a sweat and build reflexes. Remember the old adage: "Get in shape to play the game, don't play the game to get in shape."

A simple conditioning program will go a long way in losing extra pounds and sharpening the reflexes. A speed bag helps reflexes as well as upper body stamina.

Practice

Practicing and learning the track is a good way to help prevent accidental spins. Be aware of your surroundings at all times and do not get too close to the other karts. As the driver gains experience he will be more

Practicing will give you a chance to follow other drivers and prevent being tangled in their incidents. Remember; look where you want to go, not where you are going.

capable of gauging his driving ability. After a few races what once would have been a hazardous move will become a smooth one worthy of admiration. The best advice can be summarized with the statement: "When in doubt, don't."

Flags

Learn the flags and attend drivers' meetings before the race. The drivers' meetings will often cover some of the track regulations and where the flag stations are located. Follow instructions. The flags are meant to be used and observed without question. Getting the black flag does not mean the worker does not like you; it may mean the kart is on fire, or you simply forgot your neck brace. Do not take your frustration out on the workers for something you did wrong.

Other flags such as the yellow mean to slow down and do not pass at the incident. Not many drivers need to be reminded to go when the green flag drops. The checkered flag does not mean you won the race. It only means the race, or practice session is over. The flags are covered in detail in chapter 9 of this book.

Schools will explain the flags to the students. Keep in mind that individual clubs may have their own slant on the use and enforcement of the rules. Practice reacting to the flags while sitting in the kart at home.

The associations do not mandate rib vests, but these garments can help prevent broken ribs in an accident and they prevent bruises from the bumps in the seat. It is OK to take additional safety measures even if the rules do not require it.

Driving Schools

Driving schools are the best place for a novice racer to learn the basics such as kart control, and knowledge of the flags will help prevent accidents and minimize those which may happen anyhow. There he will learn the flags, driving courtesy, safety and the lines to turn a fast and safe lap. Most schools also hold sessions teaching the students how to pass and be passed safely.

Safety At The Shop and The Pits

- Clean up spills immediately
- Do not leave tools and equipment lying around
- Get help before picking up heavy objects
- Lift objects with the back straight.
- Beware of hot clutches, brakes and exhausts
- Use caution when working around safety wire and cotter pins
- Handle and store flammables with extreme caution
- Do not drink alcohol or use narcotics when working on machinery, driving or racing
- Prepare the kart properly
- Pre-tech the kart and use your own check-list
- Leave for the track early
- Double-check the truck and trailer (lights, brakes, oil, water, tire pressures, mirrors, etc.)
- When starting an engine be sure the driver has the brake on
- Check clutch stall speed at the track, not on city streets or alleys

Safety On The Track

- Drive at your own pace
- Do not try to pass if there is any doubt that you may not make it
- Bring the kart in if there is a mechanical problem
- Be rested
- Control your emotions
- Do not drink alcohol or use narcotics (even prescription ones)
- Observe the flags and workers' instructions
- Maintain a safe distance behind the kart in front of you
- Be physically fit
- Keep your equipment well maintained

Chapter 3

ACCESSORIES
Tools, Spares, Lubricants, Transportation

A karter will need some tools, equipment, spares, chemicals, fuel, oils, and several other miscellaneous items. The lists found in this chapter can also be used to go shopping with, and they can be invaluable as a guide when loading before leaving for the track.

Accessories, Spares, Tools

This list can be used to purchase the equipment needed for the first year of karting and it can be used, less a few things like the battery charger and the rule book, to load up before leaving for the track in addition to the list in chapter 9. This list is basic

and the individual karter may find he needs some items that are not on the list. Take the list to a kart shop to check for any other needed items.

Engine, its components such as the air filter, exhaust etc. and kart do not fall in the category of accessories, but remember to load them up before leaving for the track.

Air Filters

Quality air filters, when new and clean, do not harm performance on kart engines. The quality filters can run for a whole season before being cleaned, while the others should be cleaned after each race. The K&N

Accessories in karting take on many faces. Face shields, helmet, decals and the products needed to install them and to keep them clean are accessories. The numbers are also accessories. Manufacturers are usually glad to give away helmet and kart decals.

A simple tool box to carry the tools. Allen wrenches are very important in karting as most karts use Allen head bolts. Decide if your fasteners are metric or standard before buying the tools.

Some drivers opt to run the qualifying laps without a filter. Little if anything is gained from this practice, although it certainly has not hurt multiple 4-cycle champion Rod Stewart.

filters can race several seasons before needing to be cleaned and will last many years. Engine builders have found the better air filters to generally pay for themselves in short order as they clean the air far better than the cheap units, allowing less wear and in turn permitting longer maintenance and rebuild intervals. Choose a filter based on its quality and filtering ability, not just price. The better filters do not require "socks" or foam "pre-filters."

Battery Charger

Choose a small charger with a maintenance mode. For the size batteries used with kart starters, a small 10-amp (max) charger will be sufficient. "Trickle chargers" are not chargers, as they do not produce sufficient current to fully recharge a deeply discharged battery. Battery chargers are not maintenance units and some will destroy a battery in a few days if left on the battery after it is fully charged.

Batteries will last much longer if charged properly. Most importantly, recharge them immediately after the race. Use a good charger and maintenance device like this "Battery Tender" available from JM Racing in Arcadia, California.

Chain and Chain Breaker

Chain is typically available in boxes of 114 links, and in 10-foot rolls. Be sure the chain

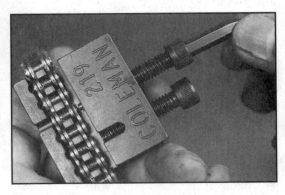

Coleman Products manufactures this nifty chain breaker. Use a good quality tool. It will last a long time and will pay for itself in fewer broken chains and less aggravation.

matches the pitch of your sprockets and driver. Purchase a good chain breaker of the same pitch as your chain. Cheap breakers tend to wear after some time and they can damage the chain.

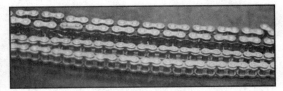

Chain comes in several sizes and quality. Find out what size chain your kart is equipped with before making the investment. Make sure your chain breaker and gears match the chain.

Gas Can and Funnel

It is a good idea to use metal gasoline containers. The plastic jugs used by many racers are not as fire resistant as the metal types and they are more prone to leakage. You can

These fuel jugs are very inexpensive and can be purchased at most hardware stores. Metal containers are safer and keep the fuel fresh longer.

buy five-gallon "Jerry Cans" at large hardware stores. Remember a spout to pour the fuel. A long neck funnel and a filter cover are advisable.

Kart Stand

A kart stand will make things easier on your back when working on the kart. Kart stands come in the folding type and the rolling models. The rolling stands are used to wheel the karts to the starting grids and they often include a shelf on the bottom to carry the starter and other tools. Choose a rolling stand with large tires and wheels.

Kart stands come in many different configurations. Get one with large wheels and one that can be folded. Inflatable tires are not a necessity and they need to be inflated on a regular basis. A tray on the bottom is helpful to carry the starter to the pre grid.

Spark Plugs

Most engines use a different length (reach), thread size and diameter and heat range of spark plug. Additionally, some classes may require a certain heat range of spark plug depending on the engine modifications, weight of the class and the fuel being used. Two-cycles run spark plugs different from those used on four-strokes. In the beginning any brand of spark plug will work, as long as it is the proper reach, heat range and thread style. Your engine builder or kart shop can best advise you on this subject, as it also involves some local considerations.

Stopwatch

For the first few races, a stopwatch may be a luxury. One will be needed eventually, but get a simple watch with a replaceable battery. A wristwatch with stopwatch function will also foot the bill in the beginning, but these usually do not have the ability to time

back-to-back laps. In this event, two watches would be necessary. Get a good stopwatch. The cheap ones are not worth the money and you will end up buying another one soon. Keep a close eye on your stopwatch, as they are easy to lose. Keep a spare battery.

Starters

Most karters use some type of electric hand-held starter to start their kart engine. The battery in these units needs to be recharged after each event and maintained between races to prevent its degradation. See chapter 12, "Maintenance", for more information on caring for batteries.

Electric starters are used almost universally in American karting on 2- and 4-cycles alike. Bringing a spark plug wrench to the pre grid is a good idea. This tool made by EJ's Creations includes a spark plug socket, a wheel wrench and a piston stop.

It is easy to confuse one starter from another at the pre grid. Place your kart number or name on your unit, so your help and other karters can easily identify it. Placing a phone number would also be a good idea in case you do forget the starter.

Tach/Temp Gauge

A good tachometer and temperature gauge would be a good idea to have even in the beginning. You will have to get used to using this instrument eventually. These gauges are

A simple tachometer and cylinder head temperature gauge will be sufficient for the beginning sprinter. Learn the basics first and keep an eye on the pocketbook.

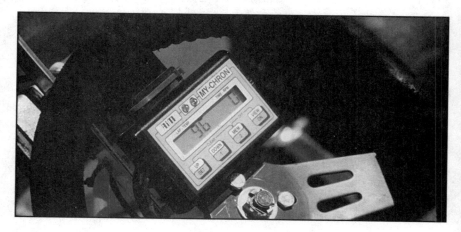

indispensable if you plan to win races eventually. Get at least a cylinder head temperature (CHT) meter. Ideally, a CHT and EGT (exhaust gas temperature) and a tachometer combination gauge will come in handy and the price for the three-instrument combo is not much more than the single or double one. Again, get something reliable, with modern electronics and with good repair facilities. Keep spare batteries.

Transponder

Transponders are little "black boxes" a bit larger than a deck of cards that are installed on the karts and which send an electronic signal to the computer in the scorers' booth. Each time a kart equipped with a transponder goes by the beam it records the kart number, its last lap time, and its position in the race. Not all clubs use transponders and not all clubs have transponders for rent. Check in advance with your club if they use the system and if transponders are available for rent or if one can be purchased. To be on the safe side check the battery before each race or better yet install a new one before each race.

Most clubs use transponders to score the events. The unit sends a signal to the timing tower each time the kart passes by the beacon. The computer saves the data and it is retrieved at the end of the race. These systems keep track of positions and time.

Chemicals and Lubricants

The local kart shop probably carries most of the products needed for the shop and track. You can obtain some items like hand cleaner, silicone gel, thread lockers, and spray paint from hardware and auto parts stores. Use the following checklist when loading for the track.

- Air filter cleaner and oil
- Alcohol fuel lubricant (methanol classes)
- Brake fluid
- Chain lube
- Clutch oil
- Engine oil
- Fuel
- Hand cleaner
- Wheel bearing grease

Lubricants

Synthetic lubricants are becoming the standard in karting as well as in all the other forms of motorsports. Remember that four- and two-cycles use vastly different oils. Some racers using methanol in four-cycle engines also add some fuel lubricant to the alcohol. Alcohol does not hold the same

On the steering wheel of this kart is a tachometer and engine temperature gauge combination. Below is a timer which self actuates each time the kart passes by a beacon. These units save the data for downloading after the practice or race. Novices can wait before buying these devices.

lubricating properties as gasoline does, and without lubricant it can cause rapid wear of the cylinder and rings in four-cycle engines.

The choice of the lubricants (for the engine, gearbox and clutch) as a novice should be based on the understanding that performance is not paramount, but longevity, economy and reliability are. Some karters still use castor oil as a lubricant. This product was the best available many years ago but the new crop of kart engines and tuning techniques often create temperatures far surpassing castor's thermal abilities and resistance to wear. This is most relevant when castor is mixed with pump gasoline with oxygenates.

Fuel

For practice, you can use good premium pump gasoline. For racing, commercial gas will throw off the tech inspector's meter and get the driver disqualified from the race because of the oxygen-bearing chemicals included to reduce emissions. Commercial gasoline could be used if the driver knows he is not going to finish near the top of the field or if he does not care about the points. Commercial gasoline is not consistent enough from one manufacturer to another and from region to region. In addition, in some areas, fuel is formulated to prevent cold starting problems; this could cause serious starting problems to a kart engine. Pump gasoline can cause detonation if the engine is run hot or the carburetion lean.

Fuel Storage

Gasoline and methanol should be stored in metal containers, in cool (sixty degrees Fahrenheit), steady temperatures. The heating and cooling of the fuel cause condensation and degradation. Fuels should be used up as quickly as possible once the container has been opened to prevent moisture from entering. Do not use plastic cans for fuel storage. Plastic breathes and it allows moisture to enter, and even the opaque jugs allow some light to penetrate. Light and particularly the ultra-violet rays of the sun cause the lead and manganese to drop out of the solution.

Basic Tools

- Clutch tools
- Compression gauge
- Feeler gauges
- Spark plug wrench
- Tire pump or air tank
- Tire pressure gauge
- T-handled Allen wrenches (metric or U.S. depending on chassis and engine). Snap ring pliers, screwdrivers, tape measure, wire cutters, needle nose pliers, pliers, files, hammer, hack saw and blades, extensions, a small and a large adjustable wrench. Box end/open end combination wrenches and socket set in either metric or standard.

The tote trays make nice little tool boxes. If you race with friends, it is a good idea to paint your tools to tell them apart. These boxes are easy to carry to the pre grid.

Compression Gauge

Invest in a good compression gauge. The type that can be screwed into the spark plug hole will be more convenient so the engine can be cranked while the gauge holds itself into the head. These gauges can be pur-

chased from tool supply houses and tool trucks.

Clutch Tools

Do not use makeshift tools on the clutch. Purchase the tools made for the clutch on your engine. Kart shops and engine builders typically carry the tools and the instructions on how to use them. Most disc clutches require a large wrench to hold the aluminum weight support. The three tools most needed are the clutch puller, the clutch wrench to hold the aluminum weight support and Allen wrenches to remove the drain plug to drain the fluid, to remove the cover and to access the adjustment screws. Chapter 7 of this book covers the basics of clutch adjustment.

Safety Equipment

The book "Karting! A Complete Introduction" from this publisher covers this subject in detail. Safety is not an area where one can skimp. Get what is best for you and purchase equipment that will satisfy the rules of your club and association. Remember to use the checklists in this chapter to load all the safety equipment before leaving for the track.

Personal Items

Karting is an outdoor sport. The elements can have a strong effect on your level of

A threaded compression gauge is installed in this US820. Note how the spark plug is grounded and the carburetor is held wide open. If you use a hand-held compression gauge, make sure to ground the spark plug far away from the spark plug hole.

enjoyment. The following list will help in making sure the necessities like helmet are not forgotten, but it will also assist in making the day more pleasurable. Use this list to load up also.

- Change of clothes and warm clothing
- Helmet and face shield
- Ice chest, ice, drinks, food
- Medication, eye drops, glasses etc.
- Paper towels
- Rain gear
- Suit, helmet, neck collar, gloves
- Sun shade
- Towel and hat
- Wallet, credit cards, check book etc.
- Map and directions to the track

- Jets (four-cycle)
- Lead
- Numbers and panels
- Plastic tie straps
- Ratio Rite (two-cycle)
- Rule book
- Spark plugs
- Stand
- Starter and battery
- Stopwatch
- Tape measure
- Throttle cable and clamps
- Tie-straps
- Tires
- Tire pressure gauge
- Transponder
- Other

Lead is a common staple in karting. Keep a small array of five and ten pound blocks at first. Know your overall weight before going out to the track.

Loading Check-List
- Battery Charger
- Chain
- Chain breaker
- Clutch tools (see kart shop)
- Cotter pins
- Driving apparel
- Duct tape
- Fire extinguisher
- Fuel and jug
- Funnel and filter
- Gears

Tow Rigs and Trailers

For your first few outings, you will not need much more than a small van or station wagon to take your equipment to the track. Later, you can invest in a small trailer or box van. If you do not plan to spend complete weekends away where your belongings would need to be locked, an open bed pick-up truck would be sufficient.

Several companies manufacture small trailers purposely built for karters. These are ideal for those who want to travel in style and safe from theft. Small properly rated utility trailers are also up to the task. When investing in a trailer, get one that is professionally built, sturdy and safe.

Do not try to transport your equipment in a vehicle not designed for the purpose. Overloaded vehicles are dangerous, and the cargo may tear-up the interior and vice versa.

A good tire pressure gauge will be invaluable. Do not skimp on these. The cheap ones are woefully inaccurate and unreliable. Get a unit with a rubber covering to keep the mechanism from being banged around the toolbox and store it in a safe location.

Small trailers like this one are not very expensive and make life a lot easier. Equipment can be locked and kept out of the elements. Note the spare tire mounted outside the trailer to save interior space.

Chapter 4
PREPARING THE CHASSIS
and Basic Handling Set-Ups

Speed comes with experience, practice and testing. The first outing to the track should be one where the novice learns the very basics of karting rather than having to work on the kart and hunt for parts and tools. Safety, comfort, reliability, and confidence are far more important at the first race. Speed can be the least important factor at this point and safety must be the leading criteria. Set up the kart so it will not require any work and is comfortable to drive. Proper set up will reduce fatigue and allow full concentration and focus.

Visual Inspection

When at the track keep a list of repairs. This will make your maintenance schedule much easier and it will save much valuable time. Use the following list to inspect the chassis and its components:

Welds: Inspect all the welds on the chassis and its components. Chassis flex while turning and passing over bumps can place a lot of stress on the welds. The major source of cracked welds is at the base of the axle bearing hangers and at the steering supports. Spindles and spindle brackets are also prone to cracks.

Seat Struts: The seat struts can crack at their base and on foreign chassis the welds can crack where they meet the chassis. Also, ensure that the bolts are tight. Check the lower seat mounts near the steering support. They help support the seat and if they are loose the seat or the mounts can crack. On American karts with bolt-on seat struts, it is a good idea to install the struts with two bolts in the seat to alleviate side flexing and reduce breakage at their base.

Too much traction, or too narrow a track can cause the kart to "two-wheel". See text to correct this condition, before the condition corrects you.

Inspect the welds at the base of the steering supports. Look at the belly pan and its mounting points which can crack.

Steering and Mounts: Inspect the lower steering mount, as it is prone to breaking. Heavy drivers who hang on the steering wheel, sticky tires and long steering shafts can cause a lot of stress on the steering supports. Inspect the steering shaft, steering wheel and hub for any looseness.

Tie Rods and Tie Rod Ends: Look at the tie rods to see if they are bent. Hold the tie rod ends between the index and thumb, and pull on the ends to check for undue slack. Turn the steering from end to end to check for bind and look for bends in the steering shaft.

Spindles: Grab the front wheels from the top and the bottom and wiggle them. Check for any slack in the spindle bolts and the wheel bearings. Look at the welds on the spindle as they can crack and break. Spin the wheels to check for warpage or rough bearings. Check the wheels for cracks and dents.

Grab the front wheels as shown in this photo. Wiggle the wheel and note any sloppiness. Replace worn bearings.

Bodywork: Inspect the bodywork for tears and cracks. The side pods and nose cone can contact the track and wear through. Look at the sidebars to see if they are bent and check the side pods to see if they are damaged. Bend up the side pod supports if they have been rubbing on the track

Belly Pan: The belly pans can crack from vibrations and from hitting rocks. Do not mount lead weights on the pan as the mass can cause the aluminum to crack and break off. Inspect the fasteners and replace them if they are worn out. The easiest way to work on the bottom of a kart is to turn it on its rear bumper.

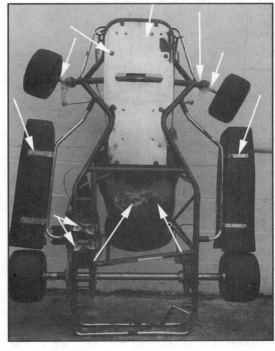

The best way to work on the bottom of a kart is to stand it on its rear bumper. There you can inspect the welds, the bottom of the seat, the floor pan, the bottom of the brakes and the spindles.

Axle and Bearings: Check the axle for bends by turning the rear wheels. A bent axle will not turn true or the wheels will turn out of round. Pull on the rear wheels to check for side play in the bearings and cassettes. Check the wheel hubs for tightness.

Cotter keys must be of the same length as their notch. If the notch is too long the key can slide out and allow the hub to turn freely on the axle.

Ensure the axle keys cannot slide out from under the hubs. This can allow the key to slide away from its hub and leave it without support. If this happens under the brake rotor, it can spin on the axle and the kart will be without brakes.

Seat: Inspect the seat for cracks and wear on the bottom where it may have dragged on the track. Remain seated in the kart for several minutes and note if it needs adjusting for comfort or to reach the controls more effectively. If you have already taken the kart out, the track notes should reflect if the seat was comfortable and if its position allowed you to reach the controls comfortably. Try the pedals to ensure there is enough movement in the ankles. The sitting position should permit the arms to bend at about 90 degrees. The seat should provide rib support, and should allow the driver enough latitude to breathe without restriction.

Instruments: If the kart is equipped with a gauge, turn it on and see if it registers the ambient temperature. If it does not work, it may just need a battery, it may need a cable, or it may need to be repaired or replaced. The battery is the most common cause of malfunction and the cables are the second. Check that the leads do not come near the exhaust, the clutch, the chain, the ignition and the spark plug wire. If the gauge is a multi-function one, run the individual wires separately. Remember that tach cables made for two-cycle will not work well on four-cycles and vice versa.

The instrument leads are very fragile and should be installed out of harm's way. Inspect for kinks and roll the extra lengths into large loops. Keep the leads away from heat and the ignition.

Measuring Tires: Inflate the tires to their proper pressure, measure their circumference and note the dimensions. The difference in size from one tire on one side of the rear axle to the other is called stagger. Stagger is used primarily in oval track racing where the right rear tire is usually larger than the left. For sprint, run zero stagger. The rear tire size should be noted as it will be needed to calculate a new gear ratio if tires of different size are used. Use a narrow metal or a tailor's cloth tape measure for this operation.

Sprint karters do not use stagger, but measure the tires to ensure they are of equal circumference. Use a narrow tape measure or a cloth tape for this operation. Measure the tires before and after they have been raced.

Cotter Pins and Lock Nuts

Most clubs and all the American associations require the safety related fasteners to be cotter pinned or safety wired. Nevertheless, karters are encouraged to use locking nuts on all fasteners. On the other hand, racers should understand that locking nuts, safety wiring and cotter pinning do not prevent fasteners from loosening. These devices prevent the nuts from falling off if they come loose. Lock washers are of doubtful value and should never be used on race cars and engines. These are of poor quality and can easily break and cause a fastener failure. Flat washers should be used under all nuts and bolts as they even-out the load placed by the fasteners, and they prevent

The washer at the top of the tie rod end is mandated by the rules to keep the tie rod attached should the ball pop out of its housing.

damage to the paint and surfaces. Flat washers also help prevent the onset of cracks around the bolt holes.

The fasteners which must be pinned include: steering hub, steering wheel, lower steering shaft, tie rod ends, spindles, spindle bolts, pedals, brake rods, brake caliper(s), and all the ballast bolts. Some chassis may have special fasteners of their own to be cotter pinned. Some brake calipers are equipped with spacer shims; these must be wired in the calipers.

In addition, the ends of the axle need to be retained by a snap ring, or another acceptable device such as a bolt or cotter pin. This is to prevent the rear hubs from sliding off the axle should they come loose.

Installing the brake rotor and hub requires special attention. Leave the rotor and hub loose, yet snug. Center the rotor within the caliper and tighten each side of the hub, a little at a time. Then go back and tighten the rotor to the hub. If the rotor is tightened before the hub is cinched on the axle, the hub will not tighten around the axle.

A cotter pin must be installed in this type of nut to prevent it from loosening. Install the nut finger tight.

Fasteners must be drilled to allow the installation of cotter pins or safety wire. Wire cannot be merely wrapped around the bolt or pin. A good rule to follow is to never leave any fastener loose and to safety wire or install the cotter pin immediately after it has been tightened for the last time. Check the fastener tightness before installing the safety wire or pin. The fact that cotter pins or safety wire are installed should be an indication that the fastener is properly tightened.

Axle Removal

Note the assembly order of the axle components, or take a picture before disassembling it. Mark one side of each part and number them if you feel you may not remember their order and direction on the axle.

Mark the inside of the axle before removing it from the chassis with the letter "L" for left and "R" for right. Use colored paint, an engraving tool or a marking pen. If possible take a picture of the axle and its components from several angles or draw a sketch of how the components are installed and which direction they face. Especially note where the keys and key ways go and which direction the hubs were facing. Keep track of the order under which the parts came off. Reverse the process at reassembly. Inspect the bearings on the axle more closely if the kart has been raced in the rain.

When reassembling the axle first install the components that occupy the center of the axle and then work your way outward. Install the axle keys in such a way that they cannot fall out from under the hub even if it is loose. Leave the bearing cassettes, the hubs and the collars loose on the axle until final assembly.

Axle Bearings

If the axle bearings are of the shielded type, they will only need to be lightly oiled with a spray lube or thin engine oil. Set the kart on its side overnight and allow gravity to do its work. Some karters remove the seals to reduce the drag they create. This allows the bearings to get dirty very quickly and to drag. Adding oil or grease to open bearings only aggravates the situation. Open bearings need cleaning and lubricating almost every race. They should be removed, cleaned in fresh solvent and greased or oiled. Worn or dirty open bearings will cost more time and money than good, fresh sealed bearings will. The beginning karter will be better served with sealed bearings, especially in the West where the tracks are generally built on sandy, dusty terrain.

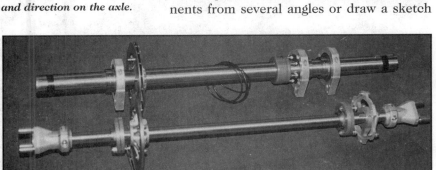

To be cleaned, axle bearings can be sprayed with carburetor cleaner spray and blown dry with compressed air. The bearings should then be sprayed with a generous coat of WD-40 and blown dry again. Then the bearings can be sprayed with Tri-Flow, a spray (works great on chains too) available at most kart shops and hardware stores.

The front wheels must not be too tight. Just right is when the spacers can be turned easily between the fingers.

Cleaning a Kart: Why?

It is difficult to see cracks and other damage through dirt. Removing the dirt entails looking closely at the parts and they can be inspected while being cleaned. The use of steam and other compressed forms of cleaning are to be discouraged for cleaning a kart chassis. The moisture can all too easily find its way into the bearings, cables, chain links and brake cylinders. Ideally, use a rag and some household spray or automotive cleaner. If the area around the engine is extremely greasy from overly generous chain lube applications remove the engine, the gear, and clean with ample amounts of carburetor spray cleaner and a mechanic's brush.

Completely disassemble and detail a used kart or one in need of serious repairs. The cleaning process will also allow the new karter to get acquainted with the kart and it will allow for close inspection of the mechanicals. Keep a notepad handy and note the items that need attention.

Brakes

The first signs of brake problems include spongy or low pedal, low pads and leaks at the master cylinder or the caliper. If the kart has been raced in the rain be extra careful in inspecting the master cylinder as water has a great affinity for brake fluid and aluminum. The three together can cause rapid and severe corrosion. If the kart is going to

be raced in rain, add some grease to the master cylinder boot to prevent moisture from penetrating. Look for leaks, spongy pedal, air in the lines and worn pads. Excessively worn brake pads can fall out (on the track) if not replaced or adjusted in time. Inspect the rotor for cracks, breaks and warpage. Set the master cylinder so the lever does not end up over ninety degrees from vertical when the pedal is applied.

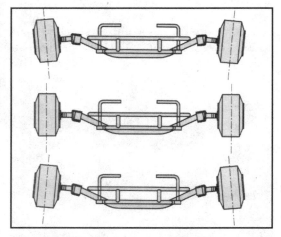

Positive camber

Zero camber

Negative camber

Seat, Steering and Pedal Positions

Think in terms of a triangle formed by the pedals, the hands and the seat. Each driver will have his preferences but nobody likes driving with the seat too far back as the pedals and the steering become difficult to reach. The seat positioning needs to be looked at from two perspectives: the angle of the back, and the fore and aft location. The angle of the seat back affects the reach of the hands and the angle of the arms, and it dictates the position of the head. Furthermore, this also affects the height of the seat bottom. The fore and aft location of the seat dictates how well the feet will control the pedals. Both settings control the front to

The best test the brakes can pass is the simple pedal pressure test. Pull on the pedal and hold it for a few seconds. The pedal feel should remain firm and steady. If in doubt, rebuild the whole system.

To bleed the brakes on a kart remove the plug on the master cylinder and install a squirt bottle in the hole. Open the bleed screws on the caliper (s) and squeeze the bottle until the fluid coming out of the bleeders is free of air. Tighten the bleed screws before releasing the pressure from the bottle or air will be sucked in the system.

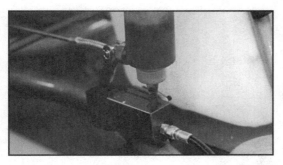

rear weight distribution which is the most important consideration in the handling of the kart.

Have the driver sit in the kart and hold the steering wheel in the way which feels most comfortable, generally at four and eight o'clock. Turn the wheel both ways. If the arms were at about ninety degrees before the wheel was turned, the seat back is probably in the correct location. Also check that the driver's head sets squarely on his shoulders without having to look down to see forward. At this point note the accessibility to the pedals when they are fully depressed. If the legs, and, or ankles have to be extended to activate the pedals, the seat is too far from the pedals. If the driver is comfortable with the steering and hand position, but the legs are not, consider moving the pedals. If the hand position could also benefit from moving the seat forward, then do so. Also, consider the height and angle of the steering wheel. It may also need to be relocated.

Lifting the front end of the kart by the bumper can do a quick check for a bent chassis. The two front wheels should come off the ground at the same time.

Prep Check List

Use this list between races:

- All fasteners
- Axle bearings, hubs and keys
- Brakes, pads and fluid
- Chain tension and condition
- Cover any sharp edges
- Engine mounts tight and good condition

- Numbers and number panels
- Safety equipment
- Seat, belly pan and bodywork
- Sprocket alignment
- Steering links and bolts
- Throttle linkage
- Tire pressure and retention
- Tools, accessories and spares
- Wheels tight
- Wheel and axle bearings
- Wires secured and out of the way

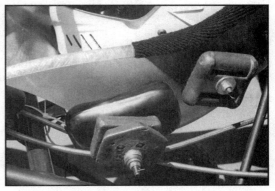

Install lead weights to the seat or on the frame, not the floor pan. On the seat, use a large washer on the inside to prevent the bolt from tearing through, particularly on the thinner seats.

Tech List

Cotter pins or safety wire should be installed only after the fastener has been tightened the final time. Check and/or cotter pin the following.

- Axle ends
- Ballast
- Brake caliper, master cylinder, and rods
- Chain guard
- Front wheels
- King pin bolts
- Pedals
- Spindles
- Steering wheel and hub
- Steering shaft blocks
- Tie rod ends

Wheel Alignment

Wheel alignment refers to the geometry of all four wheels as they relate to the chassis and the ground plane. Axle alignment and front-end toe are examples of wheel alignment geometry. Toe refers to the alignment of the front wheels in relationship to each other as viewed from the top. The term toe-in is used when the leading portion of the front wheels run closer to each other than the trailing portion of the wheels, as seen from the top.

Caster is not easily adjusted and the new karter should concentrate on the other chassis tuning parameters rather than play with the caster. At this stage, if the caster is askew, it may be best to take the kart to a shop which specializes in your chassis brand and have the caster reset. If it is not far off, live with it for now. Refer to your chassis manufacturer's specifications to set the toe on the front end of your kart.

Setting The Toe

Front-end toe must be set last if the caster and camber have been readjusted. Follow this procedure to set the toe on your sprinter:

1— Set the kart on as flat a surface as possible.
2— Center the steering as closely as possible
3— Loosen the locking nuts on the tie rod ends.

The solid rear axle on karts causes them to understeer entering turns. Narrowing the front track causes the weight to transfer to the outside front, thus unloading the inside rear, which allows the kart to turn on three wheels creating a differential effect. Under power, the inside front will sometimes come off the track. Emmick driver Gary Gwin shows the way at the Dixon kart track.

4— Have the driver or someone of approximately the same weight sit in the kart.
5— Lock the steering shaft in place as solidly as possible. TS Racing in Bushnell, Florida (352) 793-9600 produces a handy tool for this very purpose.
6— See photo for measuring.

To set the toe on the front end of a kart, apply a strip of tape to each tire and draw a short vertical line on each. Measure the distance between the two lines. Rotate the wheels 180° and measure the distance between the two lines again. The difference is the toe.

Simple Handling Cures

As a rule of thumb, as the weight of the class increases the chassis should be stiffer, the tire pressures higher and the rear weight percentage can be increased. Remember that most frequently, chassis handling ills can be traced to the driving, or more precisely, over driving.

Kart comes up on two wheels: This condition is also known as "two wheeling". The center of gravity is too high and, or, the track(s) is (are) too narrow. First, set the side-to-side weight distribution. Then widen the front and the rear track to the manufacturer's recommendations and then lower the lead weight if any. Two wheeling when the kart turns in one direction indicates one side is heavier than the other.

Push: If the front end has less traction than the rear, first look at the driving. Is the driver entering the turn late? Is he braking too hard or too late? Check tire pressures hot as the pressure can increase with temperature. Consider if there is too much rear weight on the chassis. Widen the rear track or narrow the front track. With hard tires, chances are that with maximum allowable rear track the kart can be balanced with weight distribution and tire pressures.

Loose: Check the tire pressures hot. Follow the opposite of the advice given under "Push".

Bogs: This is a common complaint from beginners. The problem occurs coming off corners where the engine is heavily loaded. The kart feels like it is "binding up." What the driver is feeling is a loss of power due to overheating caused by a lean fuel mixture or by a flooding from an overly rich mixture. Generally, this occurs a few laps into a race when the engine has heated and could use some extra fuel (turn out the low speed needle some), or when the clutch is set too low. An understeering condition is also sometimes confused as a "bog".

Hops: This sometimes occurs coming off corners when the steering is fully applied. The rear end generally starts the process and sometimes the whole kart bounces up and down. Try increasing tire pressures, increasing the number of seat struts, stiffening the chassis by means of the stiffeners if it is so equipped. Simply "flooring it" sometimes solves the problem.

Chapter 5
CARBURETOR
MAINTENANCE AND ADJUSTMENT
For Richer or Poorer

The carburetor can be troublesome on used engines or when the kart has set for long periods. Even newly rebuilt carburetors can require special knowledge, such as with the starting procedure particularly of engines equipped with the Walbro carburetors. Carburetors that have run on methanol require special attention. Methanol will cause considerable corrosion if it is not drained and the engine run for a few seconds on gasoline immediately after the end of the race day.

Carburetors

The carburetor most common in American and Canadian two-cycle karting engines is the Walbro WB-3 as used on the Yamaha KT100S and the HPV. Briggs & Stratton and Honda manufacture their own carburetors, while Comer, Tecumseh and US820 use Tillotson carburetors. In some classes, the stock carburetor is retained and in others, an aftermarket carburetor, generally a Tillotson, is used.

No matter which type of carburetor you run, check and adjust the following:

Return Springs: Check the return-springs on the carburetors, as they are the only means by which the throttle will shut when the driver lifts off the gas pedal. An additional return spring will prevent the carburetor from sticking wide open if the original spring fails.

Kart carburetors are relatively simple. Photo shows a Walbro. Learn the basics of your carburetor and which parts need most attention.

The plastic covers and fuel inlets on Tillotson carburetors can break. Tighten the screw gently and install the fuel line carefully. Note the hefty return spring on this Comer. Good practice on any engine.

Fuel Filter and Fuel Lines:
In addition to filtering the fuel each time it is transferred from container to container, an in-line fuel filter forms a good barrier against dirt. Check if the lines have hardened.

Run a fuel filter; it will save many carburetor problems. Also filter the fuel when you pour it in the tank.

Screens:
All the carburetors used in karting employ some type of internal screen to filter out foreign material. These screens are also a good indication of how the engine was maintained and of when the last time the carburetor was serviced.

Run Out
the fuel before storage especially if methanol was used. Gasoline remaining

Arrows point to the screens that need attention. The Tillotson on the left has a large filter. The Walbro on the right is not so fortunate. The smaller screens get plugged more easily.

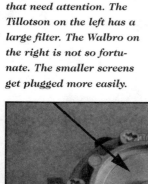

in the carburetor will stretch and destroy the diaphragms if left in for extended periods. Methanol attacks aluminum very aggressively.

Diaphragms
on carburetors should be replaced with those made of Teflon as these resist fuels more effectively than do the stock types.

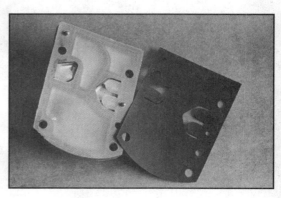

The standard neoprene diaphragm on the right should be replaced every two or three races and after each race if you run methanol. The Teflon unit on the left is far more durable, but these also require attention.

Jets:
Some four-cycle carburetors use replaceable jets. Take your jets to a shop and have them measured and marked, even if they are already marked to make sure they are of the correct size. Many racers drill out their jets and never change the marking on the head. Place your jets in a box or find some small containers like film canisters.

Fixed Openings:
Some carburetors, like the ones that come on the Briggs, have some openings that can be opened when using methanol. These should be inspected for obstructions and legality.

Plastic fuel and pulse lines harden very quickly in heat and around fuel. Use Tygon hose and replace it at first sign of hardening or cracking.

Mixture (Rich and Lean)

The terms rich and lean refer to the percentage of fuel and air mixture the engine takes in. Too much fuel and the engine is said to be running "rich." Not enough fuel (too much air) and the engine is said to be running "lean."

The fuel mixture on kart engines is generally set by the needles, and/or the jets. By turning the adjustment needle in, less fuel is allowed to enter the engine, leaning out the mixture, and vice-versa. Atmospheric conditions influence the mixture. An engine could be tuned perfectly well at sea level and then taken to a higher elevation it could run rich. The higher elevation equates to lower air pressure thus more fuel in relationship to the air.

Air Filters

Kart engines operate very close to the ground where most of the dust and debris resides. In sprint if the kart runs off the track, one gulp of dirt can destroy or severely damage an engine. Using the right kind of air filter will go a long way toward reducing engine wear and increasing rebuild periods. When cleaned, dried, and oiled properly the K&N air filters have proven to require little maintenance. For sprint racing, cleaning a K&N once a year is sufficient. When purchased new, K&N filters come pre-oiled and are ready to use. Other filters should be cleaned after each race to prevent restricting the intake.

Tillotson carburetors come in several configurations. Check your rules first and then look at your carburetor to see if it is legal.

Walbro

The Walbro WB3-A is used on the Yamaha KT100 and the Horstman HPV. Modern kart chassis and tires have evolved to such a point that engine speeds have surpassed the original design parameters of the Walbro. At the higher engine speeds many kart engines turn today, the carburetor allows more fuel than is needed for optimum performance. The excess fuel at high engine speeds was intended to cool the engines and to allow more lubrication. This is a good thing for the novice to whom optimum performance is not a primary concern, but to whom reliability, economy and longevity are of major importance.

This carburetor gives very good performance when tuned and adjusted properly. Many karters (new and experienced) have a tendency to "over-tune" their carburetor, eventually placing themselves out of contention and possibly damaging the engine. The novice should find a setting known to be rich (slightly more fuel than for optimum performance) enough to give good performance and prevent overheating and detonation. After a while, he can move the needles some to get a feel of the adjustments of the carburetor as it relates to performance and engine temperatures.

The Pop-Off Pressure

As the piston moves up and down in the cylinder, it creates pressure fluctuations,

Flex-T Company manufactures these low speed needles for the Walbro carburetors (top arrow). These are longer than the stock units are and they are flexible to prevent them from getting bent (bottom arrow points to high speed needle). Photo shows another way of installing the throttle cable.

The pop-off gauge is installed to the pulse line outlet on the carburetor and a small amount of spray lubricant is applied to the metering needle. Pressure is built up into the carburetor with the pump and the reading (the pop-off) is read on the gauge when the needle pops off its seat.

The metering diaphragm pin must hook on to the metering lever to operate properly. Novices often forget this. Ensure that the pumper diaphragm cover is tight, or it will leak air and fuel, and this is not good.

which are transferred to the carburetor via the pulse line to the pumping diaphragm. The diaphragm pumps the fuel and introduces it into the carburetor through the inlet needle valve. The inlet needle valve spring regulates the rate of flow of the fuel depending on its tension. Pop-off setting is measured in pounds-per-square-inch and it reflects the needle valve spring rate.

From the factory, the WB-3s are set around 12 PSI. This setting is fine for low engine speeds and to protect the engine in the event of an accidental engine over-rev. For racing, with the pop-off set below 9 or 10 PSI the engine will run so rich at low engine speeds, it will be difficult to start and to keep idling. To obtain reasonable performance from a carburetor so adjusted, the operator will require some experience not to damage the engine and to keep it operating on the track and out of the pits. If the engine was purchased used, check with the prior owner where the pop-off was set as it will dictate how the carburetor needs to be tuned and the engine started.

Starting Setups

It would be a good idea for a novice to take the carburetor to a kart shop and have it

Finger points to idle adjustment screw. Cut off part of the spring under the screw if additional adjustment is needed. The fuel pump cover and pulse line connection are visible below the idle screw.

adjusted so the pop-off is set between 10 and 12 PSI. In this position the engine will run cool, it will idle and it will make the engine more manageable at low speeds while you get acquainted with the controls and the track. This setting will also improve oil delivery to the ring and bearings and it will allow the engine to idle if the driver spins out.

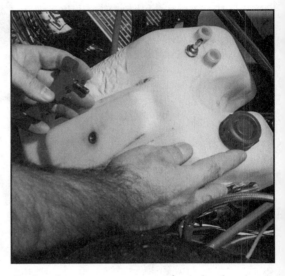

Fuel tanks are easy to remove from the chassis. Clean them out often and inspect them for residue and goop. Add a handful of small nuts and bolts, some laundry detergent and add some hot water. Shake the tank for a while and rinse it out. Allow to dry before adding gasoline.

Experienced karters set their pop-off low (8 or 9) and adjust the needles accordingly. In addition to the preceding information, several compromises must be made with a low pop-off setting:

1— With this setting, the engine will not want to idle very well to not at all. Keeping the RPM high can damage the clutch.

2— The carburetor will need to be leaned on the low speed needle during parade laps and the driver will need to reset it when the race starts. This is not an easy thing to do for a novice in his first few races.

3— When adjusted properly the carburetor will supply less fuel (lubrication) at higher engine speeds. At such time, if the operator is not well versed in tuning a carburetor, the lack of oil and the excessive heat caused by the low amount of fuel can damage or destroy the engine.

4— The engine will not run at partial throttle.

5— The clutch will require special attention in its adjustment.

Funnel filters are inexpensive and can save many headaches. These are particularly important if you run an engine with an integral fuel tank.

Yamaha:
With a high pop-off pressure (10 to 12 PSI) adjust the low speed needle out 1 to 1 1/2 turns and the high speed out 3/4 turns. Turn on the fuel (was oil mixed in the fuel?) and install the starter. When the pop-off is set at a low level (8 to 10 PSI) set the low speed needle at 2 to 2 1/2 turns and the high speed needle at 1/16th to 1/2 turn.

HPV:
For its HPV, Horstman recommends for practice and racing a pop-off setting of 10 PSI and the needles can be run at

The long tube under the Briggs carburetor pumps the fuel from the gas tank to a small reservoir under the carburetor. The short tube then takes the fuel to the carburetor. Check both tubes for dirt when inspecting the carburetor. The fuel mixture is regulated by the screw and the jet.

1 1/2 to 2 turns out on the low speed, and 1/2 to 3/4 on the high speed. When in doubt always run on the rich side (needles out more).

Briggs:
Most Briggs & Stratton classes run on methanol. In this instance pay particular attention to the carburetor as this fuel will quickly damage engines and carburetors if it is not flushed out of the system by running the engine on gasoline as soon as the race is over.

The Briggs carburetors do not require much maintenance, mainly due to their simple design. The primary points to concentrate upon include:

The Fuel Pump Diaphragm:
If the engine or carburetor were purchased used,

The Briggs carburetor is even simpler than the Walbro. Shown here is an exploded view of the pumper diaphragm and cover. Replace the diaphragm regularly especially if you run methanol. The threaded hole below the throat of this carburetor has been tapped to allow installation of a brace to prevent the carbs from breaking from the weight of the tank.

replace the diaphragm. Use a Teflon type as these resist fuels and methanol particularly better than the rubber types. The Teflon diaphragms are easily recognized by their tan color and weave pattern. These are very inexpensive and kart shops typically carry them.

The Diaphragm Cover: Surface the cover using fine sand paper and some solvent on a surface plate or other perfectly flat surface.

When removing the jet in a Briggs carburetor, use a screwdriver with a blade narrow enough to prevent damage to the threads.

The Jet and Needle: Using a half-inch box or open-end wrench remove the needle jam-nut. Once the nut is removed, the jet can be accessed using a screw driver with a blade slightly narrower than the orifice.

These holes can get plugged if the fuel is dirty. They are also tech items in most organisations.

The Mounting Bolts: The bolts holding the carburetor against the block will often need tightening. The gaskets should also be checked as they can collapse which may allow the flanges to bend. Tighten the lower tank mounting bolt and the band holding the support bracket to the tank.

Carburetor Mounting Surfaces:
The carburetor mounting surfaces can be sources of leaks. The flange at the mouth can leak air and the surface between the carburetor and the tank can leak fuel.

Inspect the area around the bolts which hold the tank on the carburetor for cracks. Check the tension on the mounting bolts and the tank support bolt.

Honda

The Honda carburetors require little maintenance. Inspect for leaks, return springs and tightness of the fasteners. A yearly rebuild is advisable. Inquire locally regarding jetting and fuels used.

Tecumseh and US820

The Tecumseh and US820 run the Tillotson carburetors. Replace the gaskets and diaphragms. Check the reeds on the 820s after every race. These can crack and break and they can weaken and lose some of their sealing ability.

Chapter 6

ENGINES
Different Strokes for Different Folks

This chapter covers the basic tuning of the engines used in American and Canadian karting. In keeping with the concept of this book, only the basic adjustments are covered. Check your local rules and regulations. Rules, elevation, air temperature all may affect the tuning and the way an engine can be tuned. Keep it simple and always focus.

Briggs & Stratton

The Briggs' simple, easy to tune, inexpensive design and its flat-head construction have made this powerplant the mainstay of American four-cycle karting. The engines come with aluminum bores (Cool Bore) and others are available with a steel sleeve (IC). For the novice the steel sleeve engine is probably more desirable as it requires less maintenance and it is more tolerant of higher temperatures.

General Tuning Parameters

• On the "stock" class engines, as a rule of thumb, run the intake valve at .004-inch and the exhaust at .005-inch. For best performance the valve lash should be dictated by the camshaft manufacturer.

• On methanol, with a Cool Bore block keep the CHT between 370 and 390 degrees. With the steel liner engines, the temperature can be elevated from 400 to 420 but do not surpass 450 degrees.

• The jets recommended for the stock classes on methanol range from 46 to 60 and more. Start with a 54 to 58. If the engine blubbers at high speed turn the needle in 1/2 turn at a time allowing a few laps for the temperature to equalize. If the needle reaches 2 1/2 turns out the jet should be replaced

Karting offers two- and four-stroke engines. The US820 is an American built two-stroke. It is reliable, easy to maintain and inexpensive to operate. Its reed valve design gives the 820 abundant power even for the experienced sprint karter.

The four-stroke engines use an inboard chain drive. This makes the use of a strong chain guard imperative to prevent injuries to the driver should the chain fail. Just above the chain guard, the air shield, which is mandatory in most stock classes, is visible. Note custom breather plate.

Use the kill switch to turn the engine off, no matter which one you run. Pulling the plug wire can damage the wire and the ignition. Hearn Competition Karting makes this custom wiring kit from aircraft wire and terminals.

with a smaller one and track test the engine. If the engine lacks power coming off the turns open the needle 1/2 turn at a time and run a few laps. If the needle needs to be turned more than 2 1/2 turns out (from closed), replace the jet with one of larger diameter and start again with the needle at 1 1/2 turns out. The CHT can also be increased by changing to a hotter plug, but only do this when the jet selection has reached the upper range (the low to mid 60s). Allow the engine a few laps to get up to temperature before deciding on the jet and needle setting. Also allow a few laps for the engine to adjust to a new setting of the needle if it was adjusted on the track. The size of the jet varies greatly depending on weather conditions and elevation.

• On gasoline start with a 38 jet. Set the carburetor needle all the way in and back it out 1 1/2 turns before starting the engine.

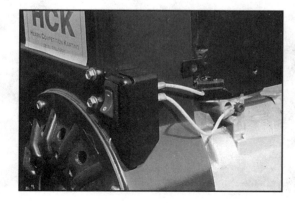

• Use a low end pipe and lower gear for your first outing. These will give you better power off the turns and it will keep you out of harm's way. Setting the clutch a few hundred RPM below the recommended speed will help in preventing clutch failure from overheating.

Comer TS-40

This engine is used in the junior classes. At 80 cubic centimeters of displacement and the light weight of the drivers, the package puts out some good speeds. Some clubs and associations require restrictors when the engine is used in the very young classes (Kid's Kart). In those classes the engine must be kept factory stock and no modifications can be done. As a two-cycle, oil must be mixed in with the fuel. The powerplant is equipped with a pull-cord, but many dads prefer the convenience of using an electric starter. The basic modifications the engine needs include replacing the filter to a K&N and removing the choke from the Tillotson HL326 or 166 carburetors which are used on these powerplants.

The Comer comes equipped with an integral gas tank, starter and exhaust. Most karters retain the hand starter and some rules require them. Note where driver's arm is positioned in relationship to the chain guard.

Set the carburetor pop-off at 10 to 11 PSI. At this setting the low speed needle can be run at 1 1/2 to 2 turns out and the high speed can be run from 1/8 to 1/4 of a turn out.

It is most important with this engine to lubricate the spark plug threads before installing it. The threads protrude in the combustion chamber and they build up carbon very rapidly. When the spark plug is removed the carbon tears up the threads. Frequent cleaning of the threads will not hurt either.

The clutch is a Comer product with 3 shoes and spring actuation. The exhaust system is a stock Comer issue and must remain as delivered to race. The spark plug to use on the TS-40 is an NGK B10HVX gapped at .028 to .030-inch.

Honda

The Honda GX160 and GX200 four-cycles are actively raced in Canada and these powerplants are gaining popularity in the States. Their main design feature is that they use a modern overhead-valve design and their carburetors are equipped with fixed jets.

The Hondas are very popular in Canada. These engines are very economical and reliable. Photo shows the air filter in foreground, the fuel tank; pull starter and exhaust pipe in the background. An integral gas tank and hand starter save a few hundred dollars.

The GXs are very reliable and durable engines. Clutches used vary based on the club and driver's preference. Where legal, most drivers use the dry disc type clutches.

General Tuning Parameters
- Use NGK BPR6ES spark plugs set at .025-inch.
- Use the stock jets for practicing if you are just starting out. The 160 uses a .68mm stock jet and the 200 runs a .75mm.
- For racing go to a .75mm for the 160 and a .85mm for the 200.
- The engines take 16 ounces of oil if the angled mount is used, and 18 ounces on the flat mounts. Hondas should be broken in with mineral oil

for two to three races before using a synthetic oil.
- The intake valve is set at .006-inch and the exhaust at .008-inch on a cold engine for both models.
- For best power replace the valve springs every two to four races.
- Optimal cylinder head temperature is 325 degrees Fahrenheit.
- Coil air gap should be set at .006 to .008-inch.

The oil sensor system should be disconnected for racing by clipping the yellow wire from the engine. This system works well until side loads cause the oil to migrate away from the sensor, causing the engine to cutout.

A bicycle drinking bottle and holder make simple catch tanks for four-strokes. Clever karter has attached the chain to the seat strut to protect it until he installs the engine.

Mufflers are becoming more widespread in karting. The Coke can makes a nifty catch can but the bicycle drinking-bottle gets the cigar. You don't see a Coke can on Jeff Gordon's car, do you?

Forget the pull starter on high compression four-strokes. Burris Racing makes these heavy-duty starters for that application.

intake and on both the Star and the H50. Do not allow the valves to run tighter than .004. This may cause loss of power and the exhaust valve can burn.

• Spark plugs generally used are the Autolite 353 for the H50 on gasoline; the Autolite 411 is used in the Star on methanol. Set the gap between .025 and .030-inch.

The square box on this Tecumseh is a fuel pump. If the engine is not equipped with its own gas tank, a fuel pump is needed to push the fuel up from the gas tank on the chassis. These are necessary on Briggs' when using a Tillotson carburetor. Choose the right pump for the engine.

Tecumseh

These American made engines typically run the Tillotson carburetors with various numbers of pumping diaphragms and bore sizes. The Tecumsehs are run on gasoline or methanol depending on the part of the country, the model of engine, the class and the club holding the events. Needless to say that the new karter racing a Tecumseh should check with the local kart club for the fuel and carburetor rules as the venturi size is sometimes regulated.

Most kart shops and four-cycle engine builders can give advice pertaining to the tuning of the Tillotson carburetors and their fuel pumps, as well as supply the parts and accessories for the Tillotson. EC Tillotson in Dickson, Tennessee is the importer and American distributor of these carburetors. The company can supply all the parts needed for the carburetors if a distributor is not available locally and it hosts a web site at: www.eccarburetors.com.

The Tecumsehs use a "flat-head" design like the Briggs & Stratton.

General Tuning Parameters

• Set the intake and exhaust valves between .005 and .007-inch for the

• Many drivers using the Tecumseh engines do not run a kill switch. The idle screw on the carburetor is turned out all the way and the engine simply dies when the driver lifts off the gas pedal. This is done to prevent engine runaway if the kart flips. The novice may want to install a kill switch until he can get accustomed with the operations and run the idle speed high

KART director Mike Baldus gets a start from tech chairman Tom Rayl. To manually start a four-cycle, pull the cord until you feel the compression. Give slight throttle. Rewind the cord and pull hard. Avoid pulling the cord all the way through as it can break.

This one-way valve is a smog valve from a 1960's car. The valve allows internal pressure to escape. However, it keeps the oil from splashing out. The overflow tube terminates into a suitable catch can.

enough to prevent the engine from dying on the track.

- Run 16 ounces of oil in the H50 and 21 ounces in the Star. With methanol the oil should be changed during a race day or a practice day. Drain the oil as soon as possible at the end of the day if you run methanol as this fuel is very thin and it tends to pass around the rings and dilute the oil. A good synthetic oil, such as Red Line's, is not as vulnerable to deterioration when mixed with methanol. Remember that engines must be broken-in with a mineral oil first, and then a synthetic can be substituted.
- Run the cylinder head temperature on the H50 if run on gasoline at 450 to 500 degrees Fahrenheit. With a Star on methanol run the CHT from 400 to 430 degrees F.

US820

The US820 engine is a 134cc two-stroke, American built powerplant. These are only available in kart shops as a complete package. They are easy to tune and to maintain, mainly due to the low RPM they turn. Yet, the 820 is faster than the stock-class four-cycles. Experienced karters say this is the least expensive engine to race in American karting.

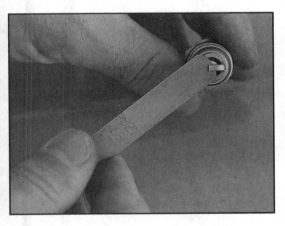

Use a feeler gauge to gap spark plugs. Plugs are not "pre-gapped" no matter what the guy at "Cheap Auto Parts" said. Gap your plugs to your engine. Check the gap before installation as it may have been banged around during transportation.

The exhaust system comes as part of the engine package and its length is variable, but most karters generally use one length as little is gained by changing the flex. The rules require the use of a standard air box to reduce noise. The 820s are run on racing gasoline only.

Many tuners adjust the engines to only run if the driver has his foot on the gas. This allows the engine to die if the driver flips the kart. This may cause the new drivers to stall out on the track; it may be a good idea for the novice to set the carburetor so the engine will idle and to install a kill switch for the first few outings and increase the idle speed a bit if the rules permit it.

The maximum useable power limit is 9,800 to 10,000 RPM. Beyond this point the engine loses power and could become damaged. There is no need to run higher than this limit; gear accordingly.

General Tuning Parameters

- The spark plug recommended for the beginner is the NGKB8 or 9 set at .030-inch.
- The carburetor is a Tillotson with low and high speed needles. The pop-off pressure is set at 9 1/2 PSI. The needles are run with the low speed at 1 1/8th of a turn to 2 turns out and the high speed is kept at 1 turn out. Adjust the head temperature with the low speed needle.
- The clutch used is a dry shoe type Ratech free of adjustments which engages between 5,000 and 6,000 RPM. This low engagement speed keeps the clutch from slipping when exiting corners, yet it allows the engine to idle in the pits and it prevents the engine from stalling if the driver loses control on the track. The clutches do not need much maintenance and can generally be raced a whole season without repair or rebuild. Occasional spring replacement is recommended.
- The US820 is a two-stroke and oil must be mixed into the fuel to lubricate the bearings and the cylinder wall. A 16: to 20:1 mixture of two-stroke oil to fuel should be used. Never attempt to operate a two-cycle engine without first mixing the correct amount of the proper oil into the fuel. Even the shortest burst without oil will cause the engine to seize.
- Run the cylinder head temperature around 450 degrees for best power. Do not exceed 490 degrees to prevent

sticking the piston. Be aware that some thermocouples read differently than others on the US820 due to its fan cooled design.

Horstman HPV

The HPV is a two-stroke and oil must be mixed into the fuel to lubricate the bearings and the cylinder wall. Like with most other two-strokes a 16: to 20:1 mixture of two-

Photo shows proper installation for ignition and its ground. Bad ignition or ground will give false plug readings and create "strange" problems like intermittent misfire and difficulty starting.

stroke oil to fuel should be mixed even if the engine is going to be run for just a few moments.

General Tuning Parameters

- Horstman recommends using a Nippondenso 29 or 31ESZU, or NGK BR9 or 10.

Clutch cover on HPV engine. These covers act in part as the third bearing in other two-cycles. The clutches on these engines are spec and are set at a low engine speed to avoid slippage and increase durability.

- The carburetor (Walbro WB3) should run with the low speed needle at 1 1/2 turns out and the high speed needle at 3/4 turn out. This setting is for a pop-off setting of 10 PSI.
- Use a 16:1 fuel to oil ratio. Some clubs may require spec fuel and/or oil.
- Cylinder head temperature should run between 330 and 370 degrees F.

Yamaha

The Yamaha KT100 is run in more fashions than the other karting engines: clutch, direct drive, "stock", modified, "Can", pipe, restricted etc. As such all the parameters one might expect cannot be crammed into a general volume such as this one. Genibrel Publications is producing a book strictly on the KT100 which includes all the engine building and tuning procedures.

General Tuning Parameters

- Most tuners use Autolite 51 spark plugs or their equivalent on the KT100 with a gap of .040-inch.
- Mix in a 16: to 25:1 fuel to oil ratio.
- A cylinder head temperature of 395 to 420 F is optimum. Do not run above 440 or the piston may seize. Use caution as some old style cylinder heads are still being used and they must run 50 to 90 degrees cooler than the new style heads. The old style head is easily recognized by its rougher casting characteristics.
- For the first few outings the new karter may want to set the carburetor with the pop-off at 10 to 12 PSI and the low speed needle at 1 to 1 1/2 turns and the high speed at 3/4 turn. This will allow the engine to idle and this setting will allow the engine to run cool.
- For racing the pop-off can be set at 8 to 10 PSI but the needles must be reset from 2 to 2 1/2 turns on the low speed, and 1/16th to 1/2 turn on the high speed. As the race progresses the driver will have to increase the fuel flow by turning the low speed needle out 1/2 to one full turn. The high speed can be leaned down slightly or it can be left alone on a hot day.
- In Super Box class, run the KT100 at 13,800 to 14,300 RPM. The Sportsman engines can turn 12,500 to

13,000. On engines equipped with an expansion chamber, consult the manufacturer for carburetor settings, peak torque (to set the clutch) and engine speeds.

General Tuning Tips

- Do not overheat the engine while racing. Air cooled engines can get overheated very quickly and easily. It is relatively easy to get an engine to warm up, but nearly impossible to cool down when overheated.
- The Japanese spark plug numbering system reflects a hotter range as their number decreases, (smaller number, hotter range). With the American spark plug numbering system an increase in the spark plug number indicates a hotter heat range, (bigger number, hotter range).
- On methanol four-stroke engines the cylinder head temperatures also react to spark plug heat range. On a "good air day" (high air density, low humidity) the jet can be quite large which will cause the cylinder head temperatures to drop. At that time a hotter spark plug can be used to increase the CHT. To decrease the CHT go to a colder plug.
- On gasoline, "reading" the spark plug is still the best way to determine the proper jetting and heat range to use. Unfortunately on methanol the spark plug does not color well and experience must come into play when tuning. Use the CHT to tune the engine.
- Using an exhaust temperature gauge (EGT) is the ideal way of tuning an engine. However, a novice should first learn how to drive and to tune the carburetor "in the ball park." More advanced books from this publisher will cover other methods of carburetor tuning, including using EGT.

Fuel

Two-stroke kart engines in the U.S. and Canada typically run on gasoline. Two-stroke oil must be added to the fuel to provide lubrication to the bearings, piston and ring. Four-cycles in the U.S. typically run on methanol. Gasoline and methanol have vastly different characteristics and cannot be interchanged. Most organizations only

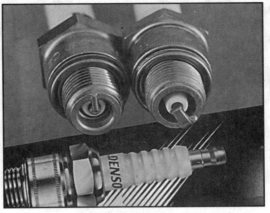

A plug with its ceramic recessed like the one on the left is colder than one with its ceramic exposed to the combustion area.

permit the use of one or the other in each class.

The fuel should be filtered each time it is poured from container to container. This is most important on engines with integral gas tanks like the Briggs and Tecumsehs where the screens on the pick-up tubes are very small and can plug very easily.

Methanol should be purchased fresh before each race. If it is stored for long periods it loses its potency and will not pass tech. Two-cycle mix should be used up within a few days, particularly if a mineral oil or castor was blended as the lubricant. True synthetic two-stroke oils have a much longer shelf life after having been blended. Plastic containers should not be used to store or transport flammable liquids. The plastic "breathes" and allows the fuel to deteriorate even faster.

Spark Plugs and Gap

The condition of the spark plug can be an invaluable indicator of the condition of the engine. It may be advisable to simply start fresh with a new spark plug of the correct design, reach and heat range for the engine and for the application such as practice or racing. The correct spark plug gap for most kart engines is .022-inch to .025-inch.

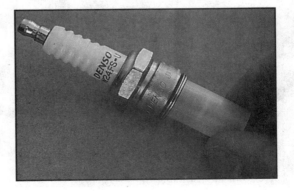

The number on the insulator indicates the thread pattern, heat range and reach (length of threaded area) of the spark plug. Keep the plastic cover in place until ready for use. Check that the threaded tip is tight. These will cause the wire to come off if they come loose.

Chapter 7
PREPARING THE ENGINE
"An Ounce of Prevention..."

Being prepared will not only save much time and frustration but money too. A day at the track should not be spent chasing Gremlins and working on the engine while others are enjoying themselves doing what they came to the track to do in the first place—race.

Whether the engine is new or used, or you are pulling maintenance between races, it should be checked and prepared before the next outing. This will also give you a baseline from which to work. This exercise will also get the new sprinter acquainted with his equipment. Used engines can be of dubious origins and may need freshening or even a complete rebuild. The engine should also be checked to insure against potential

damage. You also want the engine to be in top running order to avoid problems at the track so the driver can concentrate on his driving without the annoyances of fighting a stubborn carburetor or a dirty spark plug. Finally, engines should be in good working order to give the new driver a feel of what sprint karting is and to give him a mental base of how the engine and kart should perform.

Starting Kart Engines

All internal combustion engines require three things to operate: air, fuel and a means to ignite the charge. Furthermore, the individual elements must be in the correct ratio (air and fuel), their delivery must be exactly

Exploded view of Honda four-cycle engine shows the parts that are most likely to need attention after a season or two. Even with its overhead valve design, this engine is still very simple to operate and it is very reliable. The plate below the head is a guide plate for the pushrods.

Tighten the tip with a pair of pliers. If the tip loosens, it will fall off, potentially taking the cap with it and the engine will stall; embarrassing to say the least.

Four-cycles with long pipes use one or more supports to relieve some of the stress on the flange where the pipes can break when they get hot. Note the air filter pointing away from the heat of the exhaust pipe. The overflow tank on this kart is a windshield washer bottle.

synchronized and the onset of the combustion process must be precisely timed and be sufficiently powerful to effectively generate the combustion process. Any deviation from this process can cause the engine to not start, or to run poorly.

Starting a Two-Stroke

If you are doing this alone, set the front end of the kart against a wall and raise the back wheels so the kart will not take off when the engine starts. Preferably, have someone sit in the kart to put the brakes on. On a KT100 or HPV with a high pop-off pressure (10 to 12 PSI), adjust the low speed needle out 1 to 1 1/2 turns and the high speed out 3/4 turns (see chapters 9 and 11 for carburetor tuning for racing and for practice).

The start of a big race (or a first race) is not a good place to have an engine fail. Be prepared. Practice starting before going out to the race.

With the pop-off set at a low level (8 to 10 PSI) set the low speed needle at 2 to 2 1/2 turns and the high speed needle at 1/16th to 1/2 turn. With a high pop-off pressure (10 to12 PSI) adjust the low speed needle out 1 to 1 1/2 turns out and the high speed out 3/4 turns. Turn on the fuel (was oil mixed in the

fuel?) and install the starter. With a low pop-off you may need to turn the low speed needle out more to start the engine.

Apply the brakes, maintain about half throttle, and crank the engine. Press the throttle pedal on and off slowly. If the engine does not start, turn in (lean) the low speed needle 1/4 to 1/8th of a turn at a time and return back to the richer setting momentarily. Observe if the fuel is moving through the hose and filter

Priming the Walbro carburetors by pumping the diaphragm with a pointed object will suck some of the fuel into the line.

Starting a Four-Stroke

Follow safety precautions outlined in "Starting a Two-Stroke." On four-cycles equipped with a manual starter, pull the cord gently until the piston is on the compression stroke. Allow the cord to fully rewind into the starter and give a long, steady pull. Avoid pulling the cord all the way out to prevent damage to the starter. The engine should start after two or three pulls. Remember to turn on the ignition switch. With engines

equipped with a fuel tank under the carburetor, it may be necessary to prime the carburetor by blowing in the tank through the gas cap with a hose.

Trouble Shooting

On most kart engines, check the following if the engine does not start:

1— Fuel turned on, fresh and arriving to the carburetor (look through the filter or fuel line).

2— Gas tank breather open?

3— Is starter turning fast enough? Bringing the engine to compression stroke with manual starters?

4— Compression OK?

5— Fouled, improperly gapped or wrong spark plug?

6— Ignition defective, wet, bad ground, open or weak circuit? Is TCI grounded and operating?

7— Internal problem such as air leak (two-cycle), seized, worn or broken ring, piston or bearing?

Hearn Competition Karting makes these carburetor and pipe supports for the Briggs. The throttle cable stay is also HCK issue as well as the butterfly lever and the mixture screw adjuster.

8— Carburetor needs rebuilding?

9— Fuel or pulse line leaking air?

10—Is kill switch off? Check if it is defective by disconnecting it.

11—Broken carburetor (stock Briggs).

12—Should fuel not reach the carburetor, choke the carburetor by removing the filter and placing your hand over the throat, or, on two-strokes, prime the system by stroking the pumping diaphragm with a small pointed object. With

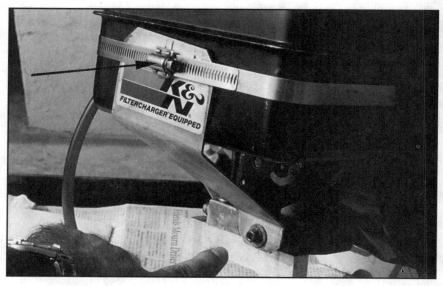

the Briggs', which have the tank below the carburetor, some karters gently blow in the gas cap with a rubber hose to prime the carburetor. Hondas and other four-cycles are often equipped with a choke mechanism. A choke can be used while the engine is cranked for a second or two, or for one or two pulls when a manual starter is used. There is usually no need to choke a hot engine. Hondas are equipped with a compression release, which makes starting much easier.

The Breather Plates: The valve stems, springs, retainers and lifters can be accessed on the Briggs and Tecumseh via the breather plate. Install a new gasket when installing the plate. Note the gasket direction, as it is instrumental in allowing the oil to drain out of the breather. Ensure that the stock breathers are installed with their drain holes toward the bottom.

Checking For Leaks: Look for air, oil and fuel leaks. Two-strokes can suffer from air and fuel leaks. The air leaks can occur at the seals around the case, and at the pulse and fuel lines. Four-strokes can leak fuel, oil and air.

Two-Strokes: Two-bangers must be closely scrutinized to avoid any air leaks into the crankcase. Such an occurrence would create a lean air/fuel mixture, which could cause the piston to seize. To test a

Check the tension regularly on the tank support bolt on the stock Briggs and the support clamp (arrow). A loose tank support is a major cause of broken carburetors.

two-cycle engine for air leaks it must be plugged at the intake and the exhaust and pressure or vacuum is installed. The internal pressure is noted and the engine is allowed to set for several minutes to an hour and the leakage can be read on a gauge, which was installed prior to the test. This test requires special plugs, which can be purchased at hardware stores and a vacuum/pressure gauge available from specialized kart shops. If you have doubts about your engine it would be advisable to simply take it to an engine builder to have it serviced. Remember: "An ounce of prevention..."

Inspect the whole length of the pull cord on four-cycles. Replace the cord or the mechanism at the first sign of wear. These are cheap enough that racers can keep spares in their toolbox.

Engine Mounts

Check that the engine mount is straight, clean and free of dents. This will help keep the engine tight on the mounts and the chain aligned.

Inspect for cracks, worn or cracked butterfly clamps and ensure the clamps are not so worn that the adjustment bolts are inaccessible. Clean the area between the mount and the engine to prevent rocks and other debris from lodging under the engine. This

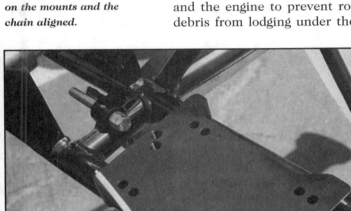

may throw the chain out of alignment and it can cause the engine to loosen on the mount. Tighten the engine to the mount with a torque wrench to prevent warping the engine case.

Manual Starters

The Briggs and Tecumsehs come with manual starters, which are normally quite reliable. The cords and the mechanisms need some attention. Look at the end of the cords where tied at the handle and look for signs of fraying along the length of the rope.

The mechanism should engage effortlessly and without slipping or catching. The pull

cords and the hand-starters are inexpensive and should be replaced at the first sign of wear or malfunction. Many karters keep a spare at all times when racing. These are quick and easy to replace at the track if needed. Most karters invest in an electric starter. These make starting faster and easier so nobody gets held up at the starting grid.

Adjusting The Valves

Check the valve lash regularly if you run a 4-cycle engine. The lash on the Honda overhead-valve is easy to adjust and should be set if you find it to be off. The correct valve lash for the Honda 160 and 200 is .006-inch on the intake and .008-inch on the exhaust. Bring the piston to top dead center on the compression stroke. Insert a feeler gauge of the recommended thickness between the rocker arm and the valve tip. There should be a slight amount of tension on the gauge as it is pulled and pushed. If the lash feels too loose, try a feeler gauge of a thousandth thicker. If it slides in the gap, the valve is too loose.

Adjusting the valves on the Briggs and Tecumseh is more painstaking. These engines share the same basic "flat-head" design, which consists of the valves being installed in the blocks without the benefit of rocker arms. Each valve is actuated directly

To check the valves on the Briggs and Tecumseh the breather cover must be removed. Bring the piston to top dead center of the compression stroke and insert the feeler gauge between the valve tip and the lifter. Adjusting the lash requires the removal of the valve and/or lifter.

by a lifter, which rides on the camshaft lobes. The valve adjustment must be made by reducing the length of the valve stem by grinding it or by changing the length of the lifters. If the valve lash needs to be increased, the karter needs to find a shorter valve or lifter, or the valve stem or the lifter tip can be ground down; this would be better left to a qualified engine shop as the valve faces should also be ground before this operation is undertaken, which requires a complete tear down.

Compression

Due to the wide range of engines, rules and modifications, it is not possible to list the recommended compression for all the engines used in karting. Check with an engine builder who specializes in your engine. Note the compression when the engine is fresh and check it after each race. A rule of thumb is a ten percent drop in compression may warrant a hone job and ring replacement. Check the piston to cylinder clearance.

Checking Compression

The compression is a good indication of the condition of an engine. Warm the engine, turn off fuel and allow the engine to run out of gas while idling. This will bleed any fuel from the combustion area and the carburetor. Remove the spark plug, install it back into the spark plug wire boot and place the spark plug on the engine so as to ground it when the engine will be turned over to check the compression, or simply run a wire from the inside of the boot to the ground. This is done to avoid damage to the ignition.

Place the spark plug well away from the spark plug hole to prevent possible fire danger from the fuel left in the combustion chamber. Open the throttle fully and install the compression gauge tip firmly onto the spark plug hole. Opening the throttle is very important to allow the engine to breathe properly and to yield repeatable figures. Crank the engine over until the pressure recorded on the gauge has stabilized. Note the figure and take the reading a second time. Check the compression after each race weekend and have the cylinder refinished and the ring replaced by a qualified engine shop. The piston in both types of engines should be replaced every three or

To check the compression run the engine for a few minutes, remove the spark plug, install or hold the gauge in the head and hold the throttle wide open. Ground the spark plug and crank the engine. Note the recording and keep it in your notes.

four ring replacements. In any case, the piston should be measured to fit the cylinder diameter.

The US820 runs reed valves which when worn or broken can affect the compression reading. Inspect the reed valves regularly and replace them at the first sign of wear or weakening. Compression readings will drop when the reeds are worn out or broken.

Two-strokes must have oil in the fuel and four-cycles must have oil in the crankcase. If either engine is run without oil, it will seize in seconds. A tag such as this one will remind you if the oil has been installed in the engine or the gas tank.

The Briggs' oil can be poured in either of these plugs. Through the lower one, with the engine level, pour the oil up to the bottom of the threads. Through the top plug, measure 15 to 16 ounces of oil.

Oil---Four Strokes

Four strokes need oil installed in the crankcase much as passenger cars do. If the engine is used, now would be a good time to drain the oil and replenish the supply with good race oil. If the engine has not been started for a long period of time, or if it was raced in the rain, it would be a good idea to install a fresh load of oil and run the engine for a few minutes, drain the oil and then replace with the oil which will be used for racing. Briggs use 16 ounces of oil, the Hondas use 18 ounces, and the Tecumsehs 16 ounces in the five-horse and 21 in the Star.

Changing the Oil

The oil must be changed at least after each race when running methanol. Some racers also change their oil at the track before the main event. Preferably, drain the oil when the engine is warm and allowed to drain for a few minutes before replacing.

All three of the four-stroke engines covered within these pages carry a drain plug on the base of the crankcase. The plugs are pipe thread square heads and they can be removed with a 7/16-inch open- or box-end wrench.

Change the oil in your four-banger often, especially if it runs on methanol. The drain plug on Briggs' and the other four-cycles is conveniently located at the base of the engine. Do not over tighten them especially if the engine is still hot.

Kill Switches

Use a kill switch on kart engines in place of pulling the spark plug wire to shut down the engine. Not only is using one of those switches more convenient, but they will also prevent you from being zapped with a few thousand volts. Using a switch also increases the life of the ignition. Pulling the plug wire causes an open circuit and the current is allowed to build, causing a potential overload and ignition failure.

One wire of the switch is connected to the secondary wire of the ignition and its other wire goes to a ground. Since the engines are seldom grounded to the chassis, it is advisable to run the ground directly to the engine to complete the circuit.

The Briggs, US820, Tecumsehs and Hondas come with their own built-in switches and a threaded hole is available on those engines to attach a ground wire. Keep in mind that an electrical circuit is only as good as its connections and its ground.

Engine Break-in

If your engine is brand new or just rebuilt, it is a good idea to break it in before racing or practicing. The bearings and the rings need to mate and the compression will increase, improving performance. The engine will run cooler when it is broken in properly. Remember to first break in any engine on a good mineral oil before using a synthetic.

General Break-in Guidelines (Two- and Four-Cycle)

- Warm up the engine at fast idle for one minute. Shut it down and allow to cool off.

Protect your investment. Cover your engine when working on it. You never know what can fall into or through it, even through the exhaust pipe.

- Warm up the engine again at fast idle for three minutes. Shut it down and allow to cool.
- At the shop, the engine can now be run for five minutes at fast idle. On the track it can be run for five minutes with short bursts of acceleration to near full throttle. Keep cylinder head temperature at twenty five to thirty percent from max allowable.
- Finally, run the engine with longer bursts of power and keep the CHT about twenty percent below maximum racing temperature.
- Check engine components for tightness between runs. Run the carburetor richer than normal.
- Engines raced on methanol can be broken-in on gasoline; remember to re-jet, or re-tune the carburetor needles when switching fuels.
- Never run the engine at full throttle for more than a few seconds at a time until broken-in.

Check the gas caps periodically. They can get plugged and the tank will draw a vacuum causing the fuel to stop flowing. Old caps come loose and fall off on the track. Keep a spare as they get lost easily.

This HPV driver displays good workmanship with the chain guard and his pipe installation.

Tank, Lines and Filters

Inspect the interior of the gas tank. Any loose residue will plug the fuel filter or the screen inside the carburetor. If the gas tank is very dirty, replace it with a new one. Also, make certain that the cap can breathe. Air must be allowed to enter the gas tank to equalize the pressure as the fuel leaves the container for the engine. A small air filter or a piece of foam can be installed at the breather hole to filter the incoming air into the reservoir. This precaution is particularly important when racing on tracks in dusty areas or when racing in heavy rain. It is also a good idea to turn the breather hose downward to prevent water from entering the tank if transporting the kart on an open trailer.

Common Problems
The most common sources of engine problems include:

- No Fuel
- Leaky fuel line
- Plugged gas cap breather
- Fouled or incorrect spark-plug
- Bad ignition
- Bad engine cut off switch.
- Popoff set low and engine will not start and idle
- Pinched fuel line
- Broken carburetor (stock Briggs)
- Engine worn and needs rebuilding
- Carburetor improperly adjusted or in need of maintenance
- Overtunning

Chapter 8

CLUTCHES, GEARS AND CHAIN
Maintenance and Preparation

The purpose of the clutch on kart engines is twofold. First, a clutch allows the engine to idle while the rear wheels are on the ground, and second, the clutch will allow the engine to accelerate before engaging to allow the kart to come off corners at a faster rate than if it were direct-drive. Another advantage is that the clutches allow the engines to use a higher gear ratio, as compared to the ratios used on direct-drive karts where the lower gearing can cause the engines to turn very high RPM at the end of the straights. High engine speeds are a serious cause of engine wear and failures.

For the first outing it would be wise to set the clutch at 400 to 800 RPM lower engagement speed than recommended and to install a driven gear with 2 to 4 more teeth than normally used on the track where the kart will first be tested. On two-cycle engines with adjustable exhaust systems, set the "flex" to the maximum of the manufacturer's recommended range. These adjustments will prevent damage to the clutch when the kart is driven at part throttle and will facilitate acceleration from slow speeds.

Clutches

There are three basic types of clutches designed for kart racing: 1) the dry disc type, 2) the wet disc clutches and 3) the shoe type units which are typically operated dry, but some are also wet.

Photo shows the three types of clutches used in karting. Left is a wet six-spring disc unit, with its cover below. Upper right is a Ratech shoe type unit and lower right is a three-spring disc dry clutch.

A Horstman wet clutch installed on a Yamaha KT100. Note the starter nut that is protruding to accept the third bearing. The three holes on the bottom plate are used to bolt the third bearing vertical plate.

sions of these clutches are available along with some special tools from E.J.'s Creations (330) 562-1651.

A single disc, six-spring dry unit mounted on a two-cycle. Check with the manufacturer for the adjustment procedure on your particular clutch. To make a Horstman clutch grab at higher RPM the adjustment screw needs to be turned in. The opposite is true for the L&T clutches.

Primarily Horstman Manufacturing and L&T Manufacturing produce the type 1 and 2 clutches. Buller Built produces a dry four-cycle unit. These clutches share a very similar basic mode of operation, but each model and each manufacturer uses a slightly different design and concept. The methods of adjustment procedures, specifications and tolerances are also different.

Since all the clutches look quite similar to the untrained eye, it would be of great interest to the karter to know the manufacturer and the model of his clutch, including the number of discs and springs, as different clutches require different maintenance methods and intervals. A heavily loaded clutch like a single disc on a heavy kart will require much more frequent attention than a multi-disc wet unit on a lighter and lower powered machine. Let your particular circumstances dictate the frequency and depth of your unit's maintenance and inspection.

The shoe type clutches come out of Ratech. These use shoes inside a drum with springs holding the shoes. As the engine speed increases, so does the centrifugal force, which pulls the shoes against the drum. The shoes then transfer the engine power to the drive gear. Blueprinted ver-

Clutch Types

The dry clutches are of an open and air-cooled design; wet clutches are enclosed and operated in special high temperature oil. Clutches come in single, double, triple and four-disc design, and other clutches such as the Ratechs utilize shoes against a drum. The friction surfaces of some of the shoe type clutches are covered with a friction material similar to the material on brake pads, and other clutches simply run bare metal shoes against the outer drum.

Clutch Selection

Clutch selection should be a part of the preparation for the first event. The fastest clutches are the lightest clutches. However the lighter a clutch is, the easier it can overheat, lose its setting and become damaged. The (slightly) heavier, wet clutches are much more learner-friendly. An improperly sized clutch for the engine or class will fail more easily than if the correct clutch had not been adjusted or maintained properly. The model of the clutch chosen should be based on the rules, the experience of the karter, and the weight of the kart and driver package, the class, the engine, and the exhaust. Following these guidelines will improve consistency, reliability, and longevity and will make for a more user-friendly experience particularly for a beginner.

Clutch life can be dramatically improved

A two-shoe Ratech mounted on a Briggs engine. These clutches are very durable and inexpensive. They are not as fast as a disc type of clutch but they are easy to maintain and rebuild.

by using the proper clutch for the weight of the kart and the power of the engine. Heavy or high-powered karts create a greater load on the clutches. Novices with these kart packages should use the two, three and four disc clutches, preferably the wet types. The single disc (especially the air cooled) clutches, and the units with the shoe mechanism are more appropriate to low power engines, lighter packages and classes where the clutch slippage is mandated by the rules. Four-cycle engines and two-cycles require different clutches due to the design of the crankshaft PTO (power-take-off), their torque output and speeds.

Some classes like the Comers, Hondas, HPVs and US820s require a spec clutch. The HPVs are equipped with a Horstman EXPD-A, and the 820s run a Ratech shoe type clutch. Some of these engine and clutch combinations run an RPM limit preset by the rules.

The manufacturers and their dealers are the best source of information to choose the clutch best suited to the individual. The book "Karting! A Complete Introduction", also from this publisher, offers many important tips on the selection of a clutch.

Clutch Setup

If you purchased the equipment used, and the clutch is a disc type, find out the following about the clutch from the prior owner or refer to the manufacturer's manual:

1— Manufacturer, and model number
2— Spring heights
3— Engagement RPM at which the engine ran best

4— Plate gap
5— Any other pertinent information such as plate thickness and which direction to turn the screws to change the stall speed (some clutches allow more slip by turning the screws in, while others operate in the opposite fashion).

If you buy a new clutch, insist on getting the service manual from the dealer. The manual often consists of a single product information sheet included in the box with the unit, but the manufacturers may offer complete service manuals. Take advice from other karters about clutches very carefully.

Clutch care

The major cause of clutch failure is overheating. Clutches overheat from excessive slippage, too much kart weight for the size of the unit, wear, low oil level or improper adjustment. The critical areas to check on disc type clutches before the first event are:

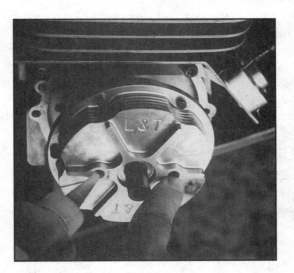

Change the clutch oil after each race. To fill the clutch with oil, open both filler holes. The Horstman clutches must have the two holes aligned parallel to the ground and the L&Ts have a line below the left hole and one above the right hole. These lines must be parallel to the ground. Fill either brand of clutch until the fluid seeps out of the overflow hole.

1— Oil level and cleanliness (wet clutches)
2— Spring heights
3— Disc clearance
4— End play
5— Engagement speed
6— Gear wear
7— Disc and floater wear

Maintenance and Adjustments

Each clutch model has its own specifications. If you do not know the model number of your unit, call a dealer and have him send you a copy of the service manual. The serv-

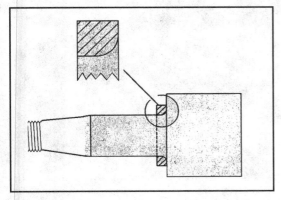

Diagram shows proper installation of the clutch spacer. The chamfer on the spacer must face the chamfer on the crankshaft or the clutch will bind.

Manufacturer's manuals are very helpful. This drawing is from L&T and shows the alignment of the reference lines to fill the clutch with oil.

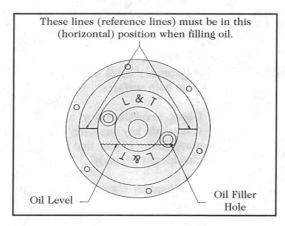

These lines (reference lines) must be in this (horizontal) position when filling oil.

L & T

Oil Level

Oil Filler Hole

ices outlined in this chapter are the basics and are not alternatives for rebuilding or replacing worn or broken parts.

Plate Gap: Plate air gap is adjustable on some models. Typically, a selection of floaters or shims is available in various thicknesses to make-up for wear and to adjust the clutch to the engine's needs. It is recommended that the novice adjust his clutch stall speed via the Allen screws.

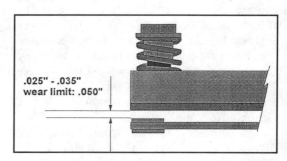

.025" - .035" wear limit: .050"

Buller Built drawing shows how easy it is to measure the plate air gap. Just use a feeler gauge.

Stall Speed: Clutch stall speed adjustment is achieved by turning the screws holding the springs in place. Most clutches include three, four or six springs and adjustment screws. Take care to adjust each of the screws an equal amount and in the same direction. Mark the clutch with a marker or piece of chalk so you can keep track of the springs that have been adjusted.

Setting The Clutch Engagement

For maximum performance, set the clutch engagement speed (stall speed) to the peak of the torque curve. For his first practice

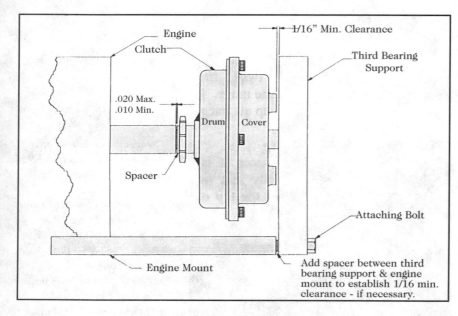

Engine

Clutch

1/16" Min. Clearance

Third Bearing Support

.020 Max. .010 Min.

Drum   Cover

Spacer

Attaching Bolt

Engine Mount

Add spacer between third bearing support & engine mount to establish 1/16 min. clearance - if necessary.

This L&T drawing shows the correct spacing between the clutch, engine and the third bearing.

Buller Built drawing shows the proper method of measuring spring height. Note that on the Buller clutches, like the Horstmans, the higher the spring height, the lower the clutch engagement speed will be, and vice-versa. Spring heights vary between clutch models and manufacturers.

Spring Height: Measure the spring height from the base of the spring retainer to the face of the aluminum support. On Horstman clutches, the higher the spring height on a given clutch, the lower the engagement speed. The L&T springs will engage the clutch at higher engine speeds the higher the springs are adjusted. The threads on the adjusting screws are 10-32; therefore, every 1/8 turn they will move .004" in all three clutches.

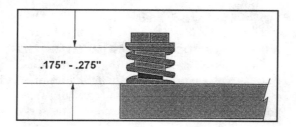

.175" - .275"

This tool from E.J.'s Creations makes installing the springs on Ratech clutches a cinch. The springs come in several tensions to regulate the engagement speed.

sessions, the novice should set his clutch 400 to 800 RPM below that figure if possible. He can readjust the clutch as his experience level improves. This will save wear and tear on the unit, as it will prevent it from over-slipping and overheating when the driver comes out of the turns at part throttle. The rules require the HPV clutch (EXPD-A) be set at a maximum of 7,000 RPM. These units are set at the factory and cannot be adjusted.

Clutch settings for kart racing engines and classes:

Settings can vary plus or minus about 200 RPM on most "stock" engines depending on temperature and air density, but a novice should set his clutch at the mid-range of the RPM listed here and be "in the ball park." For a first practice session, set the stall speed 10 to 20 percent below the recommended RPM. Very low gearing such as that used on tight tracks can benefit from clutch engagement on the lower side of the spectrum. A Yamaha with a low gear ratio could be set for example at 8,900 RPM to start. Four-cycle engines are not as responsive to this technique as are the two-strokes. As a novice, do not let the clutch adjustment distract from learning the basics. Some new drivers can get so involved with the clutch that they forget everything else. In the beginning, a few RPM one way or the other on the clutch adjustment will not make that much difference on the stopwatch; learning how to drive will be far more valuable.

Clutch Stall RPM Race Settings:

Briggs "Stock"	3,400-4,000
Briggs Limited Modified	4,400-4,800
Briggs Super Stock	3,900-4,400
Briggs Restricted Junior	2,800-3,400
Briggs Junior II	3,400-3,800
Briggs Open	4,800-5,800
(based on modifications and cam events)	
Honda	2,600-3,000
HPV	7,000
maximum (as prescribed by the rules)	
Tecumseh Star	3,400-3,800
Tecumseh 5HP	3,300-3,900
Tecumseh Modified	4,400-5,600
(varies based on modifications and cam events)	
US820 Junior	5,000-5,600
US820 Senior	5,500-6,000

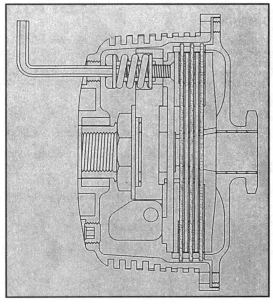

Cutaway of Horstman clutch shows the Allen wrench in the adjuster screw. Turn the wrench the same amount on each screw. Keep track of which screws were turned.

Yamaha Can (Box)	8,300-8,900
Yamaha Can Jr	8,200-8,600
Yamaha Super Box	8,800-9,200
Yamaha Pipe	10,100-10,500

The engine RPM stall speeds vary from the higher limit if at high air density and/or if the engine has been more highly modified. The lower range will be more appropriate at poorer air density, hot weather and/or if the engine is worn and/or less modified.

The plate gap and the spring heights can be checked on or off the engine. The plates can move sufficiently in the clutch to receive a quick inspection. Run the feeler gauge all the way around the clutch to look for wear spots. High or low spots indicate plate warp.

Setting the Different Clutches

To get more slip from the Horstman and Buller clutches the adjuster must be turned clockwise (tightened). The L&Ts need the adjusters turned counter-clockwise (loosened) to get more slip. Of course to lower

Use one of these wrenches to hold the clutch assembly while removing the starter nut. The crankshaft will bend if it is held from the other end. The finger points to the clutch removal tool.

the stall speed turn the screws in the opposite direction. Turn the adjusters exactly the same amount each time and keep track of which springs have been adjusted. A quarter turn each setting is sufficient to make a noticeable difference and results in about 100 RPM change.

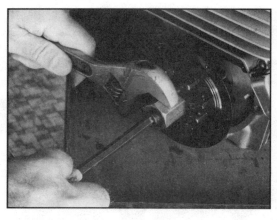

Hold the clutch tool with a wrench and turn the Allen bolt. The clutch will slip right off. Some engines have a tiny cotter key on the crankshaft which may fall off when the clutch is slipped off the shaft.

The Ratech Clutch

The Ratech is used on the US820 engines and on some four-cycle engines. The clutches generally come with two steel shoes held toward the center of the unit by spring tension. Adjustments to the Ratech clutches are accomplished by changing the springs, changing the weight and/or the orientation of the shoes.

This drawing shows the pitch, roller diameter, roller width, and pin diameter of a typical kart chain. Courtesy of Asusa Engineering.

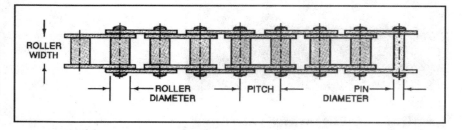

Third Bearings

The rules in some classes dictate that two-cycle engines be equipped with a "third bearing", which is a support plate for the outside

of the crankshaft on the clutch side. This mechanism reduces the vibrations and moment of inertia at the end of the crankshaft where the clutch adds to the momentum. The third bearing will increase the life of the crankshaft and the clutch and it will prevent the clutch from becoming a flying object should the crankshaft break. The bearing should be aligned with the crankshaft to prevent binding. Misalignment will cause rapid engine and third-bearing wear, and possible crankshaft failure.

Third Bearing Inspection

Remove the side plate of the third bearing and inspect the rollers by inserting a finger in the hole and turning the bearing. If the bearing is rough and catches as it is turned, it should be replaced. When reinstalling the plate slide it over the output shaft and tighten the bolts slowly and one at a time to ensure the shaft is perfectly centered. The bolts should be safety wired to prevent the side plate from falling off if they come loose. While at the track, after the kart has come back from a practice session or a race, touch the outside of the bearing and see how hot it got. If it is extremely hot, the bearing is probably shot.

Chains

The most commonly used chains in karting are the "35" and "219". The difference between the two chains is that the links in the 219 are spaced more closely than in the 35. The advantages of the 219 are that it allows the use of a smaller driving gear, and it is slightly lighter. The 219 seems to work better, and it is becoming the standard in karting. The maintenance procedure for both types of chain is the same. Always make sure the gears, clutch drums and drivers, chain breaker and chain are of the same pitch.

Chain is available in the solid pin and the split pin design. The split pin design is less expensive than the solid roller type, but it is false economy. The split rollers wear the chain and the gears faster than the solid roller chain. Using worn chains or gears is also false economy, as the worn part will wear the others.

"Breaking" a Chain

Kart chain should not be joined with a master link as used on motorcycle chain. As the master link passes over the drive gear it

Chain is available in these boxes and in bulk lengths. Buy chain in larger quantities to get the best price. Be sure you order the correct pitch of chain to fit your gears and sprockets. Do not run the chain too tightly and it should last a long time.

experiences severe centrifugal force due to the small diameter of the gear, and the clips tend to open up and slip off. Karters use chain breakers to disassemble and reassemble their chains. A good chain breaker is indispensable. A cheap, or worn out one will cause the pins to bend the plates at installation, creating an invitation to failure.

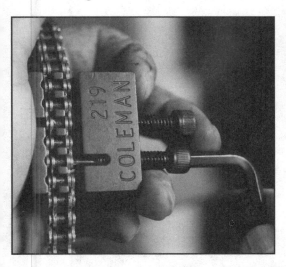

A strong chain breaker is invaluable to a karter. This unit is made of hardened aluminum and it gives full support to the links. Spray some chain lube on the pin before pressing it.

Chain Lubrication

Kart chains need internal lubrication. The rollers must rotate freely on the pins or the sprockets and the chain will wear rapidly, this process will rob excessive power.

As part of the maintenance, remove the chain from the kart, clean it thoroughly in solvent, and scrub it with a mechanic's brush. The chain should then be blown dry and allowed to set overnight. Then drop the

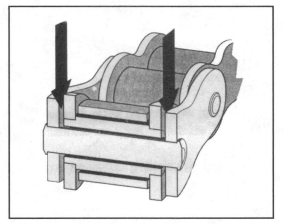

chain on its side in a can and cover it with good engine oil. Let it set this way for a day or two and the oil will seep into the chain rollers. If you have time turn the chain over

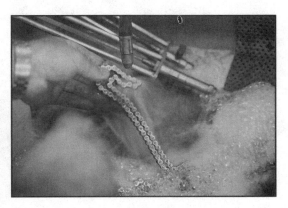

occasionally. Some karters use thick gear oil and heat up the can to allow the grease to thin so it can penetrate the rollers. Speed secrets are not on the top of the list right now.

The friction is encountered between the roller and the pin. Arrows show where the oil needs to penetrate to protect the chain. Leaving the chain in a can of oil overnight will allow the oil to seep inside the rollers. Courtesy Regina Chain.

To clean a chain use some solvent or a strong solution of laundry detergent like Tide. Let it soak in hot water for a few minutes and shake it in the bucket. Drain the water and repeat until clean. Do not use a brush as dirt particles can get pushed into the chain. Blow dry immediately to avoid rust and deposit the chain in a can partially full of oil and stir it around to get rid of the air.

To check a chain for kinks, run it over your fingers as shown in this photo. If any links are stiff, replace the chain. Also, inspect the chain visually for scratches and burrs caused by striking the track.

At the races, it is better to oil a chain when the kart first comes off the track. The chain will be warm which will thin the lubricant and it will have time to seep in between the links. When oiling the chain with sprays or squeeze bottles, lubricate the inside of the chain, where the teeth make contact, not the exterior as the oil will sling off with centrifugal force when the gears start turning.

Sprockets etc.

Sprockets (gears) are available to match the chains generally used in karting. The gears must match the pitch of the chain to perform properly or the chain will jump off the gears or, at best, the gears will wear very quickly.

Once gears have worn this far they have lost all their surface hardening. From then on, they will wear very rapidly until they completely disappear. Replace the gears before they wear this much as a bad gear will also wear the chain.

Drive sprockets come in the split and one-piece designs. For beginners the two-piece is less expensive, more easily replaced on some karts and more readily available. Two-strokes generally use an outboard power-take-off (PTO) design which facilitates the use of the one-piece gears. On four-strokes, one piece gears can also be used if the gear is not going to be changed very often.

Inspecting the Sprockets

The teeth on the gears should stand straight and not show any signs of having contacted the track. The sides of the teeth

In order to run true, two-piece gears often need a chamfer applied to their inside edge. This allows the gears to settle squarely into the hub. Note how the teeth on this gear wore from poor alignment. The tie strap keeping the gear halves together is a good idea. There is only one way to put the gear halves together. Arrow on right points to alignment mark.

should also not be worn excessively.

To check for gear warpage lay a straightedge on the frame and point one end to the gear leaving about a 1/16th-inch gap. Spin the axle and note if the gap between the gear and the straightedge varies as the axle turns. The gear or the hub should be replaced if either is warped any appreciable amount.

Aligning the Gears

First, check the axle for endplay. Any movement in the axle will negate the adjustment to the axle gear. The gears should be aligned at least on one plane using some type of straightedge resting against the drive gear. Loosen the gear hub and using a small plastic hammer tap it until the driven gear makes contact with the straight edge. This adjusts the plane as viewed from one end of the kart.

Next, check the radial alignment of the engine in relationship to the centerline of the chassis. With the straight edge still installed on the engine gear, see if it lays flat against the large gear. If the straight edge contacts the front or rear of the driven gear, the engine needs to be rotated as viewed from the top. The gear hub will probably need to be reset if the engine has been rotated to fit flush with the straightedge.

Check the alignment again after the hub and engine are tightened. It is a good idea to check the chain alignment each time the engine is removed.

The engine can then be positioned and the mount marked to indicate alignment.

To check the gear alignments run a straight edge between the two gears. Move the axle hub by tapping it gently until it is aligned with the clutch gear.

The chain guard can be installed at this time. Make sure it is wide and thick enough to meet the club rules and mostly that it will protect the driver in case the chain breaks. The chain can now be installed and adjusted.

Adjusting the Chain

Push the engine forward to exert some tension in the chain. Allow about 1/2 inch of slack in the chain and tighten the engine. Turn the axle and check the tension at dif-

of the gear butt flush together. The chain should have about 1/2-inch of play at the tightest spot in its travel.

A tight chain will not only wear itself, the gears, the clutch and crankshaft bearings, but a tight chain can also break the crankshaft. On outboard installations such as on two-cycle engines, the chain may be placed under severe tension when the wheels hit a berm or another kart; this occurrence is common with a kart in the hands of a novice driver.

To check for proper chain adjustment, turn the wheel forward and pick up the upper part of the chain. There should be about a half inch of slack. Turn the wheel and check the chain tension throughout its range. Look for tight spots. Adjust the chain to the tightest spot. Tight spots indicate the gears are out of alignment, or the axle or the crankshaft is bent.

ferent spots while turning the wheels. If there are any tight spots, the gears may not be parallel, they may be warped or the gear, or the gear halves, may not be seated properly in the hub. This is more common with two-piece gears. Check that the two halves

Starter Drives

If the kart uses an electric starter, try it out before going out to the track. Test if the shaft reaches the engine or if the side pod or bar get in the way. Also, be sure the end of the drive shaft of the starter matches the clutch nut.

Gear protectors are a good idea if you run on a tight bumpy track. Novices who will probably do some off-roading can also benefit from one of these. Note how chain is hung.

It is possible to align a chain just by sighting it down. The new tires on this kart are not going to help when the chain jumps off the sprocket in the first turn.

Chapter 9

PRACTICE DAY
Practice Makes Perfect

Entering any sporting event without any prior practice can be quite discouraging. Picture a golfer, baseball player or skier hitting the links, the diamond or the steeper slopes without some training. Karting is no different. Furthermore, in karting, practice time will allow the driver to become acquainted with his equipment as well as the driving. In motorsports, practice time, compared to other sports and activities, is quite limited even for the professionals. A day of practice, or at a kart racing school can be worth as much as a full season of racing to a first-timer. Focus.

Importance of Practicing

If you imagine all the functions the driver must perform on the track and all the data he must accumulate in just one lap, it will become clear that racing a kart takes considerable practice. A driver will look at his gauge, he will brake, listen for other karts, turn, pass, be passed, adjust his carburetor, observe flags and all this must also be performed several times per lap and often at the same time. Practice will make performing those functions instinctive, quick, efficient and safe.

Sprint karting does not always take place on wide-open tracks, some events are held on parking lots or airfields like this event at the El Toro Marine Air base in Southern California. Get used to looking over hay bales and learning the track without being able to see around the corners.

Practice getting in the kart at home. Place the left foot between the seat and the side pod and grab the top of the steering wheel.

Focus is of supreme importance in any sport and especially motorsports. Things happen literally in an instant and the driver must react accordingly. A clear mind backed-up with consistency and long hours of practice pay off in the long run.

Set the right foot on the seat bottom and move over the top of the seat. Hold yourself with the right hand over the seat back. Use caution not to lean on the engine or the air filter.

At Home Practice

Many things can be practiced at home: getting in and out of the kart, loading the kart on the stand and unloading it, reading and downloading the gauge, tuning the carburetor. Other functions such as checking tire pressures and the compression, oiling the chain, and adjusting the clutch can be practiced if the karter is not familiar with these procedures.

Slide down into the seat and extend the right leg. Pick up the left leg and slide it forward. Check that the helmet is fastened and the neck brace is on.

If you can find someone to walk a track with you before your first race you will find the experience valuable for the rest of your racing career. Remember your visual reference points, braking areas and turn-in points. Apexes will come naturally if you remember how to enter the turn.

To Get In The Kart: It is generally easier to get in the kart from the left side, away from the engine and throttle cable. Place the left foot facing forward between the side bar and the chassis. Swing the right leg over the seat and plant the right foot on the seat, taking care not to step on any cables, hoses or control rods. Slip into the seat and extend the legs to the pedals. Reverse the order to exit the kart. Take care not to push down on the air filter when getting in or out of the seat.

Loading The Kart On The Stand: This requires two people. One grabs the front fairing or bumper, while the other lifts the rear usually by the bumper. Set the stand next to the kart so it will not need to be carried over. Keep the back straight and do not pull on the kart as the other person can lose his grip. Watch out for hot exhaust systems and clutches.

Practice adjusting the carburetor, looking at the gauge and actuating the pedals at home. Set a maximum head temperature at which you would richen the carburetor. Practice that scenario.

Tuning The Carburetor and Reading The Gauge:

While sitting in the kart at home, practice tuning the carburetor and reading the gauge. Look ahead while tuning the carburetor. Wear the gloves you will wear when racing and reach over to the carburetor needles. Find a needle and turn it in and out, as you would to tune the carburetor when racing, and return the hand to the steering wheel. Repeat this exercise until you can find the needle without having to look or feel for it. Practice glancing down at the gauge and looking back up rapidly without losing concentration.

The spark plug on the left is colder than the one on the right and it has been running richer. The one on the right is hotter and its lighter coloring indicates a correct heat range and carburetor mixture. Methanol does not color the spark plugs.

Reading The Spark Plug

To read a spark plug for proper jetting look at the electrode and the interior of the plug body (on the inside of the threads). With a properly tuned carburetor and correct heat range the ceramic will be tan in color and the electrode and interior of the threads will be gray. The leaner the mixture is and the hotter the range is the whiter the ceramic will become. The richer the carburetion, or colder the spark is, the blacker it will turn. The color of the ceramic is indicative of the heat range of the spark plug while the base of the ceramic and the interior of the spark plug indicate the mixture setting. Do not attempt to tune the carburetor until you have found the correct heat range spark plug. If you run alcohol, plug reading will not be very helpful, as this fuel does not color the spark plugs. Tuning by the head temperature is more applicable when running methanol.

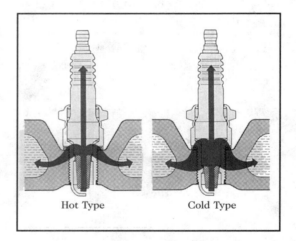

Hot Type   Cold Type

A hot plug has less ceramic adjacent to the body of the plug to dissipate heat. The cold plug on the right has more ceramic in contact with the body of the plug to dissipate the heat. Drawing courtesy NGK Spark Plugs.

Flags

Rehearse observing the flags. You might even make up some colored boards and have them waved in front of you so you can learn to react without having to think about the meaning of the flag. The best rules to follow when observing flags include safety, courtesy, sportsmanship and common sense.

Yellow indicates danger ahead, raise your hand, slow down and do not pass.

Red, the race is stopped; raise your hand and stop. Some clubs allow the karts to drive back to the start-finish line; others require them to stop on the track.

Green, the race is on, or the track is open for practice.

Black, raise your hand, slow down and return to the pits; something mechanical is amiss with the kart, part of your safety equipment is missing or your driving is hazardous and the pit marshals want to point this out to you.

Blue, a faster kart is attempting to pass. This flag does not mean you must let the other kart pass; it means that you should be aware of his presence. As a novice it is always wise to let the faster guys pass. Not only will you build a good reputation, but this way you can follow the hot shoes and learn something in the process.

White flag means last lap of practice or of the race.

Checkered flag means the race or session is over. Proceed to the scales, or the pits if in practice.

Loading Up

Bring the same parts and spares to practice that you would bring to a race. Note where everything is so it will be easier to find and note where the equipment is positioned in the truck so as to make reloading easier when returning from the race and next time out. Load up the night before and use the checklist. If this is your first time to the track, make sure you have directions. Remember the basics that you would take on any other trip such as your wallet, driver's license, credit cards, medication, glasses etc.

Be comfortable. This seat is too far back. The driver can barely reach the steering wheel and he will not be able to apply full throttle and brakes.

Load the kart stand last or load it in such a place so it can be unloaded first when arriving at the track. Keep in mind that some tracks do not allow vehicles in the pits and you may need to unload your vehicle when arriving.

Loading Check List

To make finding things easier, organize parts by categories: chain with gears, oil, brake fluid and chemicals together, safety equipment should be stored in one space, engine parts should go in a separate box, etc. Spares can go in a box of their own and tools of course in their own toolbox. Shelving and cabinets in a truck or van you may be using to travel to and from the track would make things easier. Also, go over the list in chapter 3 to ensure nothing is forgotten.

1. 9-volt batteries
2. Chain
3. Chain breaker
4. Clipboard and pen
5. Clutch tools

Loading up in a neat fashion will make the first practice much easier and safer. Being organized will allow you to focus and it will make for an enjoyable day.

A small box such as this one comes in very handy to sort carburetor parts and jets. They are available at large department stores.

6. Cotter pins
7. Duct tape
8. Fire extinguisher
9. Fuel jug and fuel
10. Funnel
11. Gears
12. Gloves
13. Goggles
14. Helmet/visor
15. Helmet and gear bag
16. Jets (four-cycle)
17. Kart and engine
18. Lead

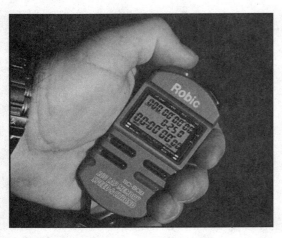

A stopwatch will be an invaluable tool when your driving becomes consistent enough to compare laps. Get a feel of the kart and the track before timing yourself. Do not spend a lot of money on a stopwatch. Something simple and easy to operate will suffice. Keep an eye on the watch as they are easy to lose or misplace.

19. Neck collar
20. Numbers and panels
21. Paper towels
22. Personal items: wallet, credit cards, medication, glasses, wife etc.
23. Ratio Rite (two-cycle)
24. Rule book
25. Shoes
26. Spark plugs
27. Stand
28. Starter and battery
29. Stopwatch (optional first time out)
30. Suit
31 Throttle cable and stay
32 Tires
33 Tire pressure gauge
34. Tire pump or air tank
35. Tie-straps

Chemicals and Lubricants

36. Alcohol fuel lubricant (methanol 4- cycle classes)
37. Brake fluid
38. Chain lube
39. Clutch oil
40. Engine oil
41. Fuel or pre-mix
42. Gear oil (Shifters)
43. Hand cleaner
44. Silicone gel
45. Solvent cleaner

Basic Hand Tools

46. Tool box: T-handled Allen wrenches (metric or U.S. depending on chassis and engine), snap ring pliers, screwdrivers, tape measure, wire cutters, needle nose pliers, pliers, files, hammer, hack saw and blades, extensions, small and an adjustable wrench. Box end/open end combination wrenches and socket set in either metric or standard. Plug wrench and feeler gauge.

At The Track Records

Note everything you think will be of interest to you in the future, such as any changes or modifications you made to the chassis, tires, engine or carburetor. Keep track of the tire pressures when cold and when the kart comes back in from the track. This will indicate a possible leak and it will indicate the amount of pressure growth from heat build-up. Note the temperature, humidity, and general conditions. Keep track of what you learned or experienced, like how the kart reacted when the clutch setting was changed, or the tire pressures adjusted. This

Focus, hard work, practice and concentration can result in great success. Many a professional race driver has had his start in karting and they too had to go to the track for a first time.

will give you references to study during the week after the practice and review your progress. Lap times are immaterial until you feel really comfortable on the track and confident with the controls, and with the tuning of the engine and the chassis.

At the Track List

Get acquainted with this list so it and the terms and procedures listed will be familiar to you on race day. Keep changes made to the kart to a minimum on your first outing. Get familiar with the equipment and the driving. Using the list will also make you perform some of the changes commonly made on karts on race day, such as changing the rear track and checking tire circumferences and pressures.

- Tire pressures cold
- Tire pressures hot
- Tire brand and type
- Tire circumferences
- Stagger
- Rear track
- Front spacers
- Corner weights
- Seat position
- Clutch setting RPM, spring heights
- Exhaust type
- Flex length
- Gear
- Lead and location
- Toe
- EGT—CHT
- RPM at end of longest straight
- Needle settings
- Spark plug appearance
- Oil
- Oil mixture (2-cycle)
- Weather

Typical Tillotson carburetor on a Tecumseh. The washer welded on the high-speed needle makes tuning on the track easier. Note the throttle bracket and angled air filter to keep heat from the pipe out of the air intake.

Install easy to reach needle adjusters. This one is long and easy to reach while at speed.

Tuning for First Practice Outing

These adjustments and settings are designed to make the kart more user-friendly; not to improve speed. This will allow the new karter more track time so he can learn the basics of driving and the tuning routines before the first race. The settings will be changed in chapter 11 to race settings. You can try those settings by the end of the practice day if you feel confident enough.

Carburetor, Walbro (KT100): Set the pop-off at 10-12 PSI. Low speed needle out 1 to 11/2 turns and the high speed out 3/4 turns.

Some karters tend to "tweak the needle" more than necessary. This usually ends up in a loss of performance and sometimes a stuck engine. In the beginning set the needles before going out on the track and only change them before the engine gets too hot.

Carburetor, Briggs: On methanol, a .050 to .054 jet can be used and the needle adjusted to tune the cylinder head temperature. On gasoline, use a one size smaller jet than recommended for racing, probably a .038 and the needle at 2 1/2 turns out.

Honda: Using gasoline, start with a .75 jet in the 160 and a .85 jet in the 200.

Tecumseh: When using the Tillotson carburetor run the low needles at 1 1/2 turns out and the high speed at 3/4 of a turn out to start.

US820: Set the low speed needle out 1 1/2 turns and run the high speed at 3/4 of a turn out.

Gearing: Use 2 to 4 more teeth on the driven gear (on the axle) to lower the ratio to match the speeds of the first few laps more closely. Decrease the number of teeth on the driven gear if the engine speed gets too high at the end of the straights. Remember the throttle goes both ways; you can always back off if the engine is over-revving.

Exhaust flex: On two-cycles with adjustable flex, install the longest flex length recommended by the pipe manufacturer. A longer flex length will shift the power peak of the engine to a lower speed. Remember to change the flex length back to the recommended setting for your application when you go race, especially if the flex length is regulated in your class.

Spark plugs: Install a hotter spark plug if your engine runs on gasoline. This will help prevent fouling during slow laps and facilitate starting.

Clutch settings: On disc type clutches, set the engagement 400 to 800 RPM lower than the recommended setting. This will prevent the clutch from overheating if during practice the kart is driven extensively at partial throttle below the normal engagement speed.

Weight distribution: Set the rear weight distribution a few percent higher than recommended for your chassis and type of racing. If the front end pushes too much, it is easy to widen the rear track. The goal here is to prevent the new driver from spinning out. These adjustments are outlined in detail in chapter 4.

At The Track

Once at the track, go to the office, purchase the passes, the insurance and register

Rest is important to keep focused and sharp. This motley crew also had the forethought of hanging their helmets to allow them to dry.

with the management. Your crew will also need to sign a release form and wear a wrist band. Ask an employee where to pit.

Unload the stand first. Since the kart is probably taking most of the space in your vehicle, unload it next; you will now have more space to unload the rest of your equipment if you wish. If you have a sun shade set it up next. Some tracks do not allow vehicles in the pits so all your boxes and equipment may need to be unloaded.

Procedure

With the kart on the stand, spray the chain, and check tire pressures. Look at your notes as a final check for any last minute reminders. Place the kart on the ground. Before starting the engine, install the fuel, and with a four-cycle install the oil.

Put on the driving suit, helmet, gloves and neck brace. Start the engine with the brake on. Once the engine has fired-up allow your assistant enough time to remove the starter. Approach the track entry and have assistant wave you out when safe.

First Session

Take five or six easy laps. Do not try to go fast. Get acquainted with the feel of the steering, the brakes and the general sensation of a kart. Note if the seat is comfortable and the pedals and steering wheel are easy to reach. In a straight, look down at the temperature gauge and make a mental note of how easily it can be read.

Keep the engine RPM above the clutch engagement speed; you will feel the clutch engage with a light bump in the back of the seat. When the clutch is slipping, the engine

Observe the better drivers on the track. Note their lines, braking points and apexes. You will probably find that most take the same lines and clip the apexes closely and in the same place each lap and they use the whole track coming off the turns.

will maintain the same pitch. When the clutch engages the engine will sound like it is accelerating. Return to the pits, let the engine and clutch cool down. Note your findings on the notepad. Go out as many times as necessary in 5 to 10 lap sessions until you feel comfortable on the track.

In between sessions, with the engine cooling, sit in the kart, turn on the temperature gauge and practice looking down at it, and looking back up in front of you by moving the eyes only. Once you feel comfortable with this procedure, reach over to the carburetor and turn the needle in 1/8th of a turn. Place your hands back on the steering wheel, look at the gauge. Look forward and turn the needle back out 1/8th of a turn. Practice this routine until your hand finds and adjusts the needle without hesitation. Reset the needle before going back out.

After coming back from a practice session, sit down and go over the track in your mind. Take notes of where you need to improve or practice. Note things like: "Go in one slower", "turn in two later", "brake later in four", etc.

Second Session

Learn to read the instruments and adjust the carburetor and clutch. Ask other drivers if they would mind allowing you to follow them for a few laps and maybe even practice passing. If you went to a driving school, now would be a good time to practice some of the moves you learned.

In the second track session work on the lines, the braking points, the apexes etc. Learn to feel the clutch engaging and work on watching the instruments. Keep working those elements in the subsequent sessions and try resetting the clutch to get a feel of how the setting changes the behavior of the engine.

Between Heats and Pre-Race Check List

- Air cleaner fastened
- Axle endplay and bearings
- Ballast secure
- Brake fluid, brake operation, pads etc.
- Clutch adjustment and oil
- Chain tension
- Chain lubrication
- Clean helmet and face shield
- Electrical connections and wires
- Engine mounts tight
- Exhaust system
- Fairing and bodywork
- Front end tight
- Fuel lines and filter
- Instruments and battery
- Note any changes, adjustments or repairs in logbook
- Number panels and numbers
- Oil level (4-cycles)
- Overall cleanliness
- Refuel
- Seat, floor and bodywork
- Spark plug clean and heat range
- Steering fasteners, mounts and rod ends tight
- Throttle operation and linkage
- Tire pressures and wear
- Tire circumference
- Wheels tight

Chapter 10
RACE DRIVING BASICS
"Hell Hath No Fury Like A Tire Scorned"... Had Shakespeare Raced Karts

The most basic principle of motorsports competition is to drive as fast as possible to accomplish the lowest possible lap time. This chapter covers the basics that will lay the principles to eventually approach this goal. "Approach" is the key word in that sentence as there is no such thing as the perfect lap. Certainly, as a novice (and a novice is a racer who is still learning the basics) setting your goals too high would be unrealistic and detrimental to the learning process. Right now, we simply want to learn the basics of race driving so we can learn how to approach the perfect lap.

The Self

Like in most other sports, confidence in motorsports usually determines the level of competence and the race finish position of the drivers. Driving a race car, or kart, is almost purely mental. If you believe you can make a pass or other move, you will. If you are not sure or you know you can't, you won't. Self-confidence comes from practice and time. Then, time and practice hone the skills.

However, as a karting novice you likely have had no practice, no seat time and no race time. This does not mean that you will

Focus, hard work, practice and concentration can result in great success. Many a professional race driver has had his start in karting and they too had to go to the track for a first time.

Seat time develops confidence. Confidence develops skills. Skills hone reflexes and reactions. Scott Cramer, Flatout Group driver, represents the epitome of confidence under pressure.

have no self-confidence. The day-to-day feelings you have about yourself, and general beliefs you hold will carry through into your race driving. Reaching some level of confidence when facing a new sport or situation, first requires belief in oneself.

Control of Emotions

A good race driver can take a slow corner slow and a fast one fast. Going slow is one of the most difficult things to learn in motor racing, and it is the factor that will decide which drivers will finish a race without leaving the track or kissing the wall. Those that do usually do not win the races and they do not turn good qualifying times. Going too fast or braking too late or too hard into a corner scrubs off a lot of speed that should be carried into the turn to be used to exit with the maximum of momentum as possible. The controlled driver applies the brakes, turns, accelerates at the proper time, and performs all these operations very smoothly. The emotional driver brakes too late and too hard, consequently he ends up turning late, with excessive steering angle, and out of the fast line. A controlled driver is a safe, fast driver.

The start of a race can be emotion filled for the new driver. Stay in your position and just follow the driver in front of you. Chances are you will be starting near the back with other inexperienced drivers. Look well ahead.

Positive Thinking

"You are who you think you are." "Whatever the mind can conceive, it can achieve." These statements carry into motorsports as well as other sports and everyday life. Set some goals—valid, positive goals. At first, set goals that are within your grasp within a short time, even the same day. For example, aiming for the lap record on your first day of practice or the first race is not a valid goal, while it is positive. Achieving a certain level of comfort in specific areas, such as taking the lines and apexes properly is a more realistic approach for a novice, even one with prior racing experience.

It is not whether you win or lose, it is about improving each lap, each race, each day. A driver cannot improve if he does not believe he can.

Baseball players have drills they follow: batting, fielding, throwing etc. Each part of the game is practiced and analyzed. Each part of your game can also be dissected and worked on, so you can learn it segment by segment. Set some drills to follow while on the track. Make up your own list of things to work on while driving, such as taking lines, braking points and apexes. Go out on the track and work those drills during practice and test days.

Most importantly set positive goals: "Turn in at the bush," "Use visual fields," "Keep the eyes moving". Tell the brain what you want it to do, not what you do not want it to do. "Don't turn until the bush," "Don't just look ahead" are examples of negative goals.

Fear

Fear is a normal reaction to unknown surroundings or events. In racing conditions, a complete lack of fear would be an irrational response. Constant fear (on or off the track) is also a sign of some type of problem the driver should come to grips with. Fear is a signal from the brain telling us to reconsider our surroundings. If you feel fear in the kart, you have probably exceeded your limits. Start slow and work up to a level of comfort and progress from there. Uncontrolled fear can lead to anger.

Anger

Anger is an extension of our fears. If another driver is angry, you will have the edge over him, but watch out for him on the track, as fear has a way of coming out at the worst moments and in the most inexplicable forms. If your fears turn to anger, pull into the pits and collect your thoughts. Remember that as in any competitive sport, in karting some drivers fear getting beat or showing their lack of talent or abilities, or simple lack of self-confidence. The schoolyard bully, for example displays anger to hide his feelings of low self-esteem and his own fears.

Focus and Concentration

Those who saw the movie "Rocky" are familiar with the expression "Eye of the Tiger." One gains this look from extreme focus and concentration. In karting, total awareness and concentration allow the subconscious to learn from repetition. Distrac-

Focus and concentration begins long before the green flag drops. Drive the track in your mind while waiting at the pre-grid.

tions such as rambunctious friends, loud music and unnecessary conversations can cause loss of focus. Some drivers may appear distant or even unfriendly at times; but this is usually a result of their deep concentration and focus on the task. Just try talking to a football player during a game!

On the track, the mind should concentrate and focus on exactly what it wants to do and prepare for it ahead of time. Complete concentration will allow using the visual fields to their maximum extent by programming the brain with the coordinates needed to implement the operation the driver wants to perform.

Focus and concentration will help you learn more than any other factor. No matter what happens in the beginning of your career, and each and every race is new knowledge gained. Nobody can take away what you learned, it is yours to keep forever (almost). If you have read this book until this point, you understand why the word "focus" is emphasized.

Dealing With People

Dealing with people often requires some self-restraint. Occasionally some drivers will display a bit of bravado when they spot a newbie and they may drive a bit rough with him. It is usually a part of the initiation process and they do not mean any harm but it is sometimes difficult to restrain your emotions and not speak out.

Tech inspectors can be overworked and sound a bit caustic. Try to be as calm as you can be and as cooperative as possible. You cannot win a debate with the tech guys by arguing. In fact, you probably cannot win by not arguing either.

Learning the Track

Learning the mysteries of your local track is invaluable. Hopefully, a school is available there so you can learn the basic lines, braking points and passing areas. A club practice can also be helpful as experienced drivers will be available to show you the tricks of the trade. Observing a few races from various vantage points can also be helpful when learning a new track.

Walking the track, especially with an experienced driver, can be very helpful. Understanding the lines as they relate to the subsequent turns is difficult when first entering the sport. When walking the track take some written notes of reference points such as apexes, braking areas and rough spots on the track that should be avoided. Note if the inside of the turns is rutted, where the "marbles" end-up and if the corner can be driven low or if it will require a wide line.

Flags

The flags are the only method of communication the workers have with the drivers. Each flag has a meaning and each has its own response. The vigor with which the flags are waved or pointed and their display, such as furling or full waving also carry a meaning. The "yellow" for example, indicates danger ahead; a standing yellow flag indicates the kart is probably off the track, yet extra caution should be exercised. A yellow flag being waved vigorously indicates a serious obstruction on the track. Memorize where the flag stations are located around your track and glance at the person manning the location well before the turn. Review the flags before the event.

Practice makes perfect. Even the professional drivers test and train. Karters should practice as often as possible to improve. Here Patrick Long takes his first world championship race checkered flag.

Driving

LLL: The three "L" principle is composed of: look, listen, and lines. This principle is the basis for learning kart racing. Always look ahead and to the inside of the turns you are about to enter, listen for another kart which may be trying to overtake you and work the line the best you can as it is the most important part of driving a race kart. The other segments within those principles

Do not worry about who is behind you. On some tracks, it is possible to see the karts chasing you when going around tight turns. In this turn, the driver can see the whole track. Look ahead and use visual fields.

will come naturally as you perfect the lines to each corner.

Implementing the three "Ls" smoothly, without abrupt movements in the controls, separates the karters from the champion karters. Smooth driving requires planning before acting on the controls. Establishing points for the driver to concentrate on will prepare the brain in telling the body where to turn the wheel, where, when and how much to apply the brakes and the throttle. Visual fields are key in negotiating a racing maneuver smoothly and effectively.

Visual Fields

"Watch where you are going", "Keep your eyes on the ball," "Keep the head down when swinging the club;" no matter which sport one plays, inevitably the eyes and position of the head lead the way. The eyes and head direct the muscles toward what they are looking at. In other words, if you want to hit something, look at it. If you want to avoid it, look where you would rather go.

Watching where you are going in motorsports is not always the best approach. Watching where you want to go is usually more productive. If at the end of a long straight for example, the driver looks straight ahead, he will not be able to make the turn. If he looks at the braking point and then the apex, he will be looking where he wants to go, not where he was going. Professional drivers follow these principles but they are so accustomed to following them that they do not realize they are doing it.

The lines span the visual field the driver's eyes should cover when approaching a turn.

The proper approach, entry, apex and exit of a turn are directed by those principles. Fix your eyes on the braking point, then the turning point, the apex and the corner exit. Each time the mind will instruct the body to take the kart to that location, just as the baseball hitter will direct the bat to the ball by keeping his eyes on it. Furthermore, the eyes will fan across the track to go from point to point and reconnoiter the track for places to pass, karts and obstacles to avoid and the visual field will draw the path of the kart on the track, directing it toward the lines and apexes.

The visual field of the approach of a turn should also include the exit of the turn. There, a kart may have spun; some flagmen have the habit of waving the yellow flag at the exit of a turn after the incident, instead of the entry where it can be seen by the drivers and allow them ample time to slow down or take the necessary evasive maneuver. As the eyes fan the track, the brain develops "Visual Reference Points."

Visual Reference Points

The broad visual fields should also encompass visual reference points (VRPs). VRPs include any object or track irregularities such as cracks, ruts or discoloration. A bush on the side of the track, a tree or other landmark can be used as a visual reference point. A small black rubber patch often builds up at the entry of the turns where the groove develops, and can be used as a VRP. Signs on the track wall can also serve as reference points. Avoid using non-permanent objects such as cones, people and shadows as VRPs, as they will move or disappear all together.

VRPs are used to initiate braking, turn-in or even driving straight as when coming out of a turn and cutting across the track. Rely on visual reference points to remember escape routes and run-off areas in case you are bumped out of the track, or if you run out of brakes. The key to finding visual reference points is to find the point where you want to perform the operation such as braking, turning etc.; sometimes none are available and sometimes none are necessary.

From this position, the visual field covers all six sections of the upcoming turn.

Lines

The essence of race car driving is defined by the placement of the car throughout the race lap. This applies not only where the kart is located currently, but as a prerequisite to where it will be in the ensuing turns. The "line" determines the trajectory of the kart through each turn and series of turns. Its proper implementation is more conducive to fast, smooth and safe laps than

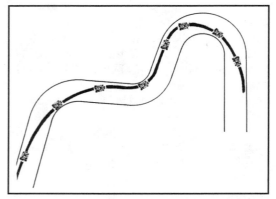

The last turn before the straight is always the most important. Taking the turns prior to the important turn will dictate the exit speed into the straight. Here the first right-hander is taken fast to scrub speed. The left turn is sacrificed to enter the last right turn late to allow for early acceleration.

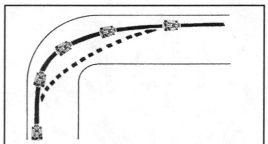

Diagram shows the rain trajectory. In the rain, the rubber laid down in the standard line will be very slippery. By keeping out of the standard line, the tires will find better traction.

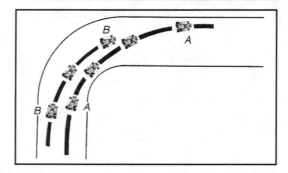

Kart "A" went under kart "B" at corner approach and possibly under braking. By the apex, "A" was occupying space "B" needed. At the apex, "A" has a clear shot to accelerate out of the turn and pass "B".

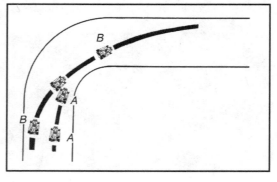

"Two objects cannot occupy the same space at the same time" Here "A" did not go under "B" far enough. "B" shut the proverbial door on "A" and continued on his merry way. It is a fine line between cutting somebody off and taking up the space he wants. Courtesy Chassis de Kart.

any other maneuver performed by a race driver. The ideal racing line is one that allows the most amount of time at full throttle and with the least amount of steering input and brake application. The line should also allow for smooth steering, brake and throttle inputs. The fastest line is not always the ideal line in racing when other karts are present on the track.

A driver can choose from three basic lines: the "early" line, the "standard" line and the "late" line. Variations of lines fall somewhere between the very late and very early lines. Each line relates to where the apex of the turn is clipped and the shape of the turn, traffic, track conditions, speed and handling of the kart. As a novice, concentrate on the standard and late lines.

Apexes

The apex of a turn is defined as the closest spot inside the turn that the kart will come to. The apex is considered the end of corner entry and the beginning of its exit. On long road race corners, the apex is not as defined as the drivers can ride the turn and the apex extends over a longer distance, making it a curved line rather than a point.

As you might have guessed by now, the line taken by the driver will determine the location of the apex in the turns and the apex will determine if the kart will come off the turn early or late. An early line is conducive to an early apex and early exit, and a late line dictates a late apex and a late exit. How these apexes are reached is quintessential to fast and safe lap times. A turn cannot be apexed early with a late line, and the driver cannot place the kart on a late apex with an early line without considerable tire scrub and slowing.

Jerry Freckelton Jr. leads the pack toward the apex of a turn at Adams kart track in Riverside California (the oldest kart track in the world). Frecky has all his might focused on that one apex. Nearly two decades ago this author photographed another young karter in the same location who took this turn in the very same fashion. Richie Hearn went on to a successful professional CART career.

Late Apex: In sprint the late apex usually creates the fastest line around a turn. The late line allows the chassis to settle into the turn, and it allows the kart to slow while turning. In sprint karting, this maneuver also allows the chassis to unload the inside rear wheel to produce a differential effect of the two rear wheels. The late line is taken even later when the turn is of a decreasing radius.

The Geometric Line: The geometric line is the fastest path through a flat-out corner. It is simply the line that would be drawn by running a compass from the center of the turn through its apex. This line places the apex of the turn near its center. This line is easy to see on television during open wheel or stock car races on true oval tracks.

Early Apex: The turns can be clipped early when passing other karts, or if the turn is of an increasing radius shape. When faced with a series of turns, the driver must consider the fact that the first apex dictates how the next turn will be taken. In a series of turns where the last turn leads to a long straight, the last turn must be approached to carry the maximum amount of speed down the straight, even if speed is sacrificed in the previous corners.

The Defensive Line: The kart is on the defensive line when it is placed where the other driver wants to place his kart to

Emmick driver Cory Gwinn approaching an apex at the Dixon track in California. Arrow points to the black spot left by the tires of the fast drivers. Cory probably aims at that spot several turns in advance. Note his inside rear tire off the track.

maximize his speed. This maneuver can be quite effective when performed properly. In the hands of a novice, it may be called blocking or, worse, a trip into the dirt.

Driving defensively at the novice stage should comport watching for the other karts, the flags and signals from the safety personnel and the staff. Again, when in doubt, don't. Play it safe, you will be the winner in the end.

Six Sections

The six sections of the line include: the approach, braking, turn-in, entry, apex and accelerating out using the whole track. All the actions should be coordinated to maximize acceleration out of the corner. The turn-in is the most important and difficult segment of the corner as its execution will dictate where the driver will begin to accelerate. Acceleration, in turn, dictates the amount of speed which will be carried down a straightaway.

In a series of turns always consider the last turn as the most important even if you have to sacrifice speed in the other turns. The first arrow in the back points to the late entry used, the second indicates another late entry and the last displays the apex.

Approach: The approach to the turn begins when exiting the last turn. If the last turn was a right-hander, the kart will exit on the left side of the track. If the next turn is a left-hander the driver should aim the kart diagonally across the track to make the track as short as possible. If the two turns are in the same direction, the driver should keep the kart in a straight line on the outside of the track. In turns forming a sequence, the first turn of the series is the approach.

Here the white line behind the kart marks the end of the approach and the beginning of the braking zone. The driver's visual field includes the entry and apex. His eyes have drawn the line in his mind and now it is just a matter of allowing the kart to go where the mind wants it to go.

Now the driver's eyes sweep over the turn-in point and the apex. In this turn, he should be able to start accelerating just after he starts to aim at the apex.

The driver's visual field includes the apex and the exit. He should be starting to accelerate right about this point while aiming for the "sweet spot". As soon as he hits the apex, he should be at full throttle and ready to unwind the steering. If he has to pull out of the throttle, or to add steering at turn exit, he probably blew the turn along the way.

The driver is aiming at the exit of the turn. He is leaving little room for error, but a novice should be more cautious. Thanks to Phil Gibbler of JM Racing for his assistance in this photo series.

While in the straight the driver can listen for another kart approaching, formulate a pass on another kart, and this would be a good time to check the gauges and to adjust the carburetor if needed. However, for the first few races, it would be advisable to set the mixture on the rich side and leave it alone throughout the practice sessions and the race.

Braking: Find your braking point. Before braking lift the right foot off the gas pedal. Apply the brake pressure gently. Release the brake pressure gradually as the steering wheel is turned into the corner. Have the brake pressure off at, or before the apex.

Novices (and some more experienced drivers) find themselves spinning out when using the brakes. Use the brakes lightly. Gentle use of the brakes is most important on a wet, bumpy, or slick track. Braking has set the stage for the turn-in.

Turn-in: The turn-in section is very important as it sets the stage for the line and the apex of the turn. If the braking was off, the turn-in will be inaccurate. Each mistake will compound until the turn is blown completely. In some turns in sprint and road racing an early turn-in can be used to protect a position.

When approaching the turn, start from the extreme outside of the track. Note how driver is already looking to the apex. By the way, do not pit at the end of a straight-away.

Generally this section of the track is the most misunderstood; this section is very important because of the number of actions which are taking place while it is being negotiated: turning, braking, rolling off the throttle and aiming at the apex. The distance covered between the turn-in and the apex constitutes the entry portion of the line.

Corner entry: This section of the turn will dictate how precisely on the apex the kart will be placed. To a fast driver, a few inches away from the ideal apex in all the turns can mean a full second on the watch. If the apex is clipped too tightly, damage or a spin can result from hitting the berm.

Phil Gibbler's right front tire is riding the thin rubber line left by the other karts. With experienced drivers, the line becomes thinner and more precise. Also, note how wide the rear of his Tony kart is. New karters need to learn to keep the rear tires a safe distance from the berms. Think ahead.

Apex: How accurately, precisely and consistently the apex is clipped separates the pros from the amateurs. As a novice, allow some breathing room between the wheels and the apex. The inside of the corners can be rough and there can be berms which if hit can cause severe damage to the chassis.

Placing the kart on its proper apex will allow the driver to accelerate as early as possible and as hard as possible. This last

Number 108, Gillard of France, takes the conventional line through the last turn of Las Vegas' Kart City. Long is taking a slightly lower line to come out earlier and to enter the next turn, also a right-hander late to get more time to accelerate earlier. Number 139, Valiante of Canada, takes an even earlier line to get a shot at Long.

point is more important in low traction situations such as on a wet track or on very hard tires.

Acceleration: Acceleration out of the corners creates the speed that will be carried down the straights. The earlier and harder the driver can accelerate the faster he will complete the straight and the easier he will be able to pass other karts. Use the whole track coming off corners.

Passing

Even in your first races, you will be passing some karts and you will be passed by faster karts. Officials may ask you to start in the back of the pack, or you may even request it. This will give the new driver an opportunity to pass slower karts and to possibly be passed again later in the race.

Passing, like the other maneuvers in auto racing, is an art; one which requires practice, concentration and planning. The easiest place to pass is in the straights. The second most common place to make a move on another driver is entering the turns.

Leave some room on the outside of the turns. Hitting berms is very hard on the chassis and the axle, and it can cause the chain to jump. Besides, it slows down the kart and can easily send the driver to do some agricultural racing.

Passing on the straights requires planning that no other kart is present on the side on which you make the move. Look, listen and plan your line (LLL). Knowing how other drivers respond will become invaluable as you progress; if you know who you are passing, you can generally gauge your speed against his and know how he will react. A late line taken by your opponent generally allows you to make a pass coming out of the turn even if your kart is slower than the kart you are trying to pass.

Passing going into a turn is generally done and is easier to execute to the inside of the kart being passed. Take an early line and brake slightly later. If the other driver does not back off, ride next to him around the turn and then accelerate early to pass him coming out of the turn. Easier said than done.

Being Passed

Following the "LLL" formula when being passed, you should already have looked and listened when possible to spot karts coming up behind you. While it is not recommended the driver look over his shoulder in the turns or straights to spot the competition, it is sometimes possible to look to the side after having exited a hairpin turn and note the karts entering the turn.

Faster karts will probably pass you on the straights or going into a turn. While it is possible to hold off a pass by using the early line, for a novice this will generally result in being passed coming off the turn. If the novice knows a faster kart is attempting a pass, signal by pointing in the direction you are allowing him to pass. This will help you make friends and influence people.

Long is leading Gibbler in this turn. Both have the advantage over the other drivers as the next two curves are to the right. The best 152 can do is hang in there and hope for a hole in the traffic.

The last turn of a series of turns is a good place to pass. 08 is preparing to put a move on 75 who is getting passed because he should have been passing number 9. It's that easy, really.

Chapter 11

RACE DAY
The Throttle Goes Both Ways
Focus, Focus, Focus

Load up at the latest the night before the event and make sure everything is done on the kart, the engine and equipment. Use the checklist in chapter 9 to load. Gas up your truck, put your wallet, credit cards, medications, glasses etc. in the truck or with your keys so nothing will be forgotten. Leave early enough to get to the track with plenty of time to register, unload, weigh, pass tech inspection, mount lead and paste numbers if necessary get a schedule and change clothes.

Once at the track, remember that this is probably your first race and you are there to learn and get through this day. Relax and learn everything you can and most importantly remember that you are there to have fun and learn. You are not going to win anyhow, so make the most of the day. You should have set some realistic goals for this event and if you feel overwhelmed, remember that the throttle goes both ways, on the kart and in your mind.

Race Day Set-Up

The engine tuning described in chapter 9 was to allow for easy starting, pit exit and for smooth acceleration off the slower turns without over-taxing the clutch. The driver could retain those settings for race day if he feels confident that he will not over-rev the engine. If the driver has some practice under his belt, he may want to change the adjustments to approach race settings. Again, retain the "practice settings" as long as you can to maintain focus on the basics and the learning process.

Walbro Carburetor KT100 Can Class:
To start, retain the pop-off at 10-12 PSI, the low speed needle out 1 to 1 1/2 turns, and the high speed out 3/4 turns. Experienced racers run the pop-off at 8 or 10 PSI but the needles must be set at 2 to 2 1/2 turns on the low speed and 1/8 to 1/2 on the high. At these settings, the engine

The first race day can be somewhat chaotic. Just do your best and learn all you can. Remember that all the professional race drivers you see on TV had a first race too. Focus.

Be prepared so you will not waste any practice time. Get to the pre-grid in plenty of time.

Try to keep your work area picked up. It will make for a safer work environment and your day will be more pleasant. The stack of tires in this photo is a reminder of why spec tire classes are a good idea for the beginner and expert alike.

will not idle. Read the spark plug or monitor the temperature gauge to tune the carburetor. On a Yamaha with the new type of cylinder head, a temperature of 400 to 425 is acceptable; 450 degrees should be the limit.

On the track, once the engine is warmed up, if you find a flat spot at lower engine speeds, turn the low speed needle out 1/8th turn at a time. For higher engine speeds do the same with the high-speed needle.

Briggs: When using methanol, in stock classes (stock carburetor) the recommended starting race jet for a Briggs is .050 to .054, with the needle at 1 1/2 turns out. On gasoline, start with a .038 jet with the needle at 2 1/2 turns out. If the engine cuts out at higher speeds, turn in the needle 1/4 turn at a time. Remember that with methanol it may take a few laps for the engine to come up to temperature and for the miss to disappear.

Honda: Start with a .75 jet in the Honda 160, and a .85 jet in the 200. Read the spark plug to determine if the jet needs to be changed.

US820: Run the pop-off pressure at 9 1/2 PSI. The needles are run with the low speed at 1 1/8th of a turn to 1 1/2 turn out and the high speed is set at 1/2 to 3/4 of a turn out. Lean (turn in) the low speed if the engine floods when coming off the turns. Lean the high-speed needle if the engine is flooding at high RPM, and turn the needle out if the engine flutters.

Tuning Tillotson Carburetors (Four-Strokes)

- Always use the Walbro four-stroke fuel pumps. Other pumps may be designed for two-strokes and will not work well on four-cycle engines.
- Some of the Tillotson carburetors are designed for gasoline, others for alcohol. Consult your Tillotson dealer for the proper model number for your application. If you encounter severe tuning difficulties it may well be that the carburetor has not been modified for your class or the type of fuel you are using.

Try to keep the practice set up for the first race. If you feel confident enough, make small changes before the race. Colin Fleming (19) and Jerry Freckelton Jr. (7) usually race neck and neck. Their set-ups are probably very similar and seldom change.

- Under normal circumstances, the low speed needle should always be turned out more than the high speed.
- Set the pop-off at 8 1/2 pounds for alcohol and 11 1/2 for gasoline.

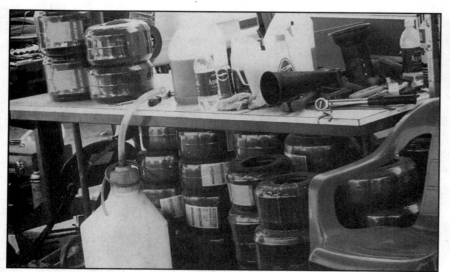

- With "stock" Tecumsehs set the low speed needle at 1 1/4 to 1 1/2 turns and the high speed needle at 3/4 to 1 1/4 turns out to start.
- On super stock engines set the low speed needle at 1 1/2 to 2 turns out and the high speed at 3/4 to 1 turn out.
- If the engine has a flat spot or bogs down leaving the pits, open the low side another 1/2 turn. Once underway, turn the needle back in 1/2 turn. Once the engine is warmed up if you still find a flat spot at low speed, open up the low speed needle a small amount at a time until the engine comes off the turns clean and crisp.

EC Tillotson USA hosts a web site with complete tuning information for all their carburetors: www.eccarburetors.com

Gearing: If you have not had any practice prior to this day, you may want to start with two to four more teeth on the driven gear (on the axle) than used by the fast guys to lower the ratio to more closely match the speeds of the first few laps. Decrease the number of teeth on the driven gear as the day progresses especially if the engine speed gets too high at the end of the straights. Remember the throttle goes both ways; you can back off if the engine is over-revving or if you feel you are going too fast for your abilities. Be cautious that the gear is not so large that it contacts bumps in the track.

Load your kart stand with the starter, helmet, gloves and every other piece of equipment you will need for the race. Hopefully, you put the kart through every test and check listed in this book.

The drivers who start at the front do not have to worry as much about spun karts. Watch out for the other guy. Drive defensively and conservatively.

Exhaust Flex: Again, if you feel comfortable with the speeds and you run a two-cycle with adjustable flex, install the flex length recommended by the pipe manufacturer for mid-range power. Remember to change the flex length back to the required setting for your application if the flex length is regulated in your class, and if it can be changed at all.

Clutch Settings: On disc type clutches, we had set the engagement 400 to 800 RPM lower than the race setting. This was to prevent the clutch from overheating if during practice the kart was driven at partial throttle below the normal engagement speed. You may wish to readjust the clutch to slip at the torque peak of the engine.

Spark Plugs: If your engine runs on gasoline install a colder spark plug than you used in the practice set-up. This will help prevent misfiring at high engine speeds and it will facilitate starting.

Weight Distribution: Set the rear weight distribution where recommended for your chassis. If the front-end pushes (understeering), add some front weight. If the kart is loose (oversteering) add some more rear-end weight. These adjustments are outlined in detail in chapter 4.

Race Procedures

Each club has its own particular methods of handling registration, and race procedures. Things may seem a bit confusing at first but by the end of the first day, you will get into the routine.

Registration

Registration staff will usually require the driver and the crew members to sign an insurance waiver, fill out an entry form that includes names, addresses and other pertinent information, and the class you will be running in. Workers may ask for the class weight. Get a schedule of events.

Drivers' Meeting

The drivers' meetings are mandatory, and they can be an invaluable source of information to a new or experienced karter. Topics such as these are often discussed at the meetings: starting procedures, safety hazards, new rules, general club news, methods of race procedure, schedule, upcoming

Some pre grid areas are small. Drivers may be asked to wait until the driver in front of you has left before you can go. This will keep the "squirrels" from scampering through the pre-grid.

events and new members are often introduced at the drivers' meeting. Some clubs have the trophy presentation for the last race at the drivers' meeting. See who got the trophies in your class. They will generally be the more experienced drivers, from whom you can learn. Try to get a pit space next to them.

Attend the drivers' meetings. You will get to meet new people and learn the "ropes" for the day. You do not want to be asked: "Weren't you at the drivers' meeting?."

Weight and Safety Inspection

Weigh the kart first even if you have weighed on another scale. Allow a few pounds for safety. On a hot day, you can expect to lose a couple of pounds or more before the end of the event.

Follow instructions. If you are held up in the pits, it is probably for a good reason. Remember this is supposed to be fun; keep it that way.

Club volunteers usually perform pre- and post-race tech inspections. They only enforce the rules. Some of those rules may sound odd at first, but if you inquire as to their meaning, they will soon make sense (usually). In any case, the kart should have been prepped at home and should be ready to clear tech with flying colors.

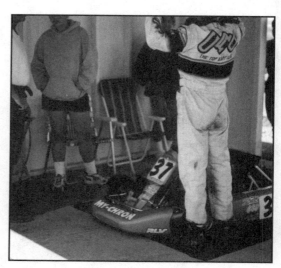

Everyone must weigh in after a race; even if you drive for CRG. Look at your weight on the scale so you will know how close you were to the limit for next race.

Tech inspection is required at all karting events. If the inspector finds something amiss on your kart, don't take it personally; the rules are the same for everybody, even if you got away with it before.

Practice

Seat time is invaluable to the new karter. By now you should have put in a day or two of private practice. If not, you may not have had a chance to race against other karts and experienced drivers. Try to stay behind some of the other drivers and observe their lines, braking points and driving techniques. Do not assume everything you see other drivers do is good driving. Work the basics and see how others work those basics.

Concentrate on driving in the practice sessions. Set the carburetor on the rich side and the gear on the lower side so you can get off the corners reasonably well without getting in anybody's way. On two-cycles run

Race volunteers are always cheerful and easy going because they are never overworked, they get paid so well and they are fed the finest in gourmet cuisine. They do not work when it is cold, hot or raining. They always smile and they always have plenty of time to consider everything they hear or see. They are especially nice when the karters do not follow instructions and argue with them.

the flex on the longer side and the carburetor a bit richer. See chapter 9 for "practice set-ups".

Qualifying

Most clubs run qualifying in different ways. Some run a 2 or 3 lap qualifying against the watch, others hold 2 heat races with pea-pick starting positions. Do not let anyone talk you into a "qualifying set-up"; these last minute plans are generally counter-productive. For now work on the driving and race set-up.

Some drivers wait as late as possible to go out and qualify to allow the track to "come

in" and for the air to cool. As a novice, this is wasted time. Go out and do your best. Qualifying can be stressful. Relax and enjoy yourself. The timed laps you will take during qualifying will encompass everything you have learned thus far. No pressure though; you have nothing to prove. If you have followed the advice in this book and spent some time practicing, you will probably end up near the middle of the pack if not close to the front.

Keep the engine set-up the way with which you practiced. Changing anything at this stage would only confuse the issue. Make changes in the second race, or go out and practice another day and try the race settings.

The Start

Sometimes races do not get the green flag on the first try. Some karts lag behind or the drivers near the front "jump the gun". At the start, the pole driver should set the pace. The drivers in the front few rows generally will start accelerating before the green flag is

Just finishing the first race will give you a great feeling of satisfaction. No matter if you finish first or last, you too will pass under the checkered flag.

Chances are that you did not have the opportunity to practice starts before your first race. Keep your cool and do not make any sudden moves. Stay behind the other drivers.

waved. It is up to the other drivers to follow. From the back, it is sometimes difficult to see what is happening at the front. If your vision of the starter and the pole position kart is blocked, simply follow the karts in front of you. If the race does not get the green, the drivers will raise their hand (usually) to warn the drivers behind them.

Once underway, try to get a feel of your surroundings for the first 2 or 3 laps. Generally, the karts that are much slower than yours will be easy to pass. If you have any doubts about passing, don't pass. This is the first race and it is a learning experience. Some clubs have a no passing rule until the start-finish line is crossed; this should have been explained at the drivers' meeting and

In the pits and on the track, races are usually started with the karts side by side. Wait for the driver in front of you to leave; remember that two objects cannot occupy the same space at the same time. Always keep an eye peeled for foreign spies wearing sunglasses.

you should have asked if you were not certain. Do not allow the noise and commotion to disturb you. Go slower than you think you should go. The proximity to the other karts will give the feeling that everything is happening more slowly than it did in practice. When possible allow some distance between your kart and the others. Maintain the same lines you practiced around the turns and down the straights, while remaining aware of the other karts that may be trying to pass you. There is a lot of excitement in a first race and it is easy to misread your speed; drive accordingly and focus.

The white flag will be displayed at the starter's station on the last lap. When the checkered flag waves, raise your hand and proceed to the scales. Keep the helmet with the kart and place the kart on the scale. The inspector will read the weight for you and will tell you "OK" or "not OK". If you finished in the top four or five positions, you may be asked to wait for the post-race tech inspection, if there is a tech inspection. Many a novice has won his first race, or finished near the top simply by attrition in the tech barn.

The Race

Some drivers may not feel confident enough to start in their earned position. It is perfectly acceptable to ask the pit marshal to start in the back. In fact, some clubs have a rule that dictates that first timers must start from the back.

Before the race starts, find out where your starting position is. The easy way to remember is to find the number of the kart that will start in front of you and the kart next to you. Remember that the kart on the pole position is on the inside of the first turn. In other words, if the first turn is a right-hander the pole position will be on the right side of the track. Get to the pre-grid in plenty of time to find your starting position. Remember to bring your helmet, gloves, neck brace, goggles and whatever else you may need to start. You will need the electric starter and a spare spark plug and wrench may be a good idea, especially if you run a two-stroke on gasoline. One last thing, if your fuel system is equipped with a fuel shut-off, remember to turn it on before attempting to start the engine— yes, it happens more often than you may think. Fortunately for those racing a Briggs, the fuel is always on.

Chapter 12

MAINTENANCE BETWEEN RACES

"A Stitch In Time Saves Nine"

Even though racing karts generally undergo strict preparation and tuning, they remain a competition vehicle utilized "at the limit." Even if the kart finished the last race without breakdown, it should be checked to prevent troubles from happening and to keep the problems that have begun from developing into a failure that can keep you out of a race or worse, cause an accident. A good maintenance schedule will save time, money and effort and it will allow the new sprinter to focus on learning the basics that are so important at this stage.

Cleaning Between Races

The pros disassemble and clean every single part of their karts after each race. As a novice, your time and resources are probably more limited and the need for a com-plete tear-down somewhat reduced, but at least remove the engine and side pods. Cleaning is an ideal way of inspecting karts and their components when they return from a race. A clean chassis can reveal cracks and other problems in the forming stages. A clean kart will be more pleasant to work on and, when you return to the track, you will not look like you just fell off the turnip truck.

General cleaning can be done with a household spray like "409" or other similar compound. Avoid abrasives such as steel wool or abrasive cleaners. Pressure sprays like those at the quarter-car-washes may be quick, but the pressure forces water and detergents into the bearings, rod ends and into threads and other holes, nooks and crannies. Rust and stuck fasteners are the inevitable results. Corrosion building inside

The axle requires more attention than any other part of the chassis. Take a picture or draw a diagram of the order in which the axle is assembled. Check if the axle is bent by spinning the wheels; see text.

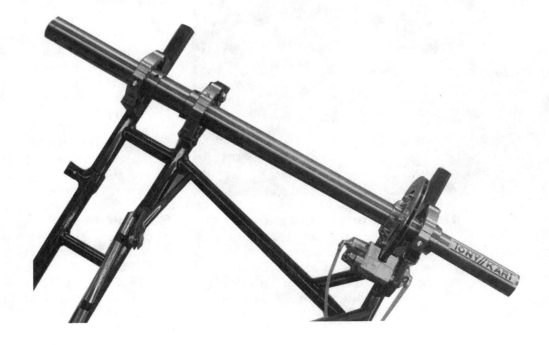

77

To clean a K&N air filter pour a small amount of the K&N filter cleaning solution in a shallow container of warm water and roll the filter in the mixture until clean. Take care not to allow the cleaning solution to enter the inside of the filter. Rinse with clean, cold water. Shake and allow to air dry. Then oil the gauze with the K&N spray oil until the filtering element is uniformly colored by the solution.

a pinhole can develop into a crack.

Areas around the chain can be heavily coated with grease (a good reason not to go crazy with the chain lube). There you can use "carburetor cleaner" and a stiff brush. Removing the engine will make this process much easier.

Visual Inspection

When at the track keep a list of repairs or adjustments you feel will be needed. This will make your maintenance schedule much easier and it will save much valuable time. Use the following list to inspect the chassis and its components. The list is written in the order in which the process should be carried out. Chapters 4 and 7 also cover the subject.

Note maintenance items that will need attention, tools or equipment which need to be purchased, repairs to the kart, engine or tow vehicle. Note ideas to try at the next event as well as driving tips such as lines or passing areas. Make a list of the items to be inspected and adjusted.

Remove engine and side pods:
This will make working around the kart much easier. If you run an engine with inboard drive, wait to remove the chain; if the axle needs to be replaced, the chain will be easier to remove with the axle off the kart.

Axle and bearings: Check the axle for bends by turning the rear wheels. A bent axle will not turn true or the wheels will turn out of round. Check the bearings by turning the axle without the chain. Worn or dirty bearings can be easily identified by their unmistakable growl.

The spindles also require a lot of attention during maintenance. Check for play in the spindle bearings and for wear in the wheel bearings. Camber and caster are also adjusted at the spindle. The washers between the spindle and the chassis are used to set the front ride height and the corner weight distribution.

Check the gear hub, the gear and the rotor for warpage: Use a straight edge on a firm location and spin the axle. If the rotor or gear hubs appear warped, check if the axle is bent. If the axle is not bent then the hubs, the rotor or the gear are bent.

Spin the front wheels: Listen for noisy bearings and look for out of roundness. If the bearings are noisy, lubricate them. If then they are still noisy, replace them. Over-tightening of the front wheels is the major cause of bearing failure. The spacers should be able to turn freely after the wheel has been tightened.

Spindle bearings: Check for play in the spindle bearings by grabbing the wheel at the top and bottom. Pay particular attention to these if you ran in the rain.

Remove the wheels: The wheels can be inspected more closely and the tires can be changed if necessary. Clean the wheels with the tires off and inspect for warpage, cracks and dents. Dents can easily develop into cracks. Minor scratches and dings can be filed smooth.

Dents and scratches on wheels can grow into cracks. A cracked wheel can explode. Note the tire rotation arrow on this tire. Arrows should point into the direction of rotation of the tire.

Welds: Inspect all the welds on the chassis and its components such as the spindles, steering supports, steering column etc.

Seat: Inspect the seat for cracks around the back, at the strut mounting holes and check the wear on the bottom where it may have dragged on the track. If you run an inboard clutch, make sure there is sufficient room between the seat and the drive gear to prevent it from cutting into the seat and to allow enough space to adjust the clutch.

Seat struts: The seat struts on some American chassis can crack at their base and on foreign chassis the welds can break where the struts are welded to the chassis.

Steering and mounts: Inspect the lower steering mount, as it is prone to breaking.

Tie rods and the tie rod ends: Look at the tie rods to see if they are bent or loose. Lubricate the rod end balls with thin oil like 5-W.

Spindles: Grab the front wheels from the top and the bottom and wiggle them. Check for any slack in the spindle bolts and the wheel bearings.

Bodywork: Inspect the bodywork for tears, and cracks. The side pods and nose cone can contact the track and wear through.

Belly pan: The belly pans can crack from vibrations and from hitting rocks. Do not mount lead weights on the floor pans as the weight can cause the aluminum to fatigue and break off.

Instruments: If the kart is equipped with a gauge, turn it on and see if it registers the ambient temperature. Test and replace the battery if necessary.

Brakes: Look under the master cylinder boot, the caliper and at the connections for fluid leakage. Feel the pedal for sponginess. Inspect the pads for uneven or excessive wear. Check that the pedal does not approach going over center or the lever on the master cylinder is not close to perpendicular with the pull rod. Bleed the system after each race. Rebuild the brakes at the first sign of trouble, or on a yearly basis. Check rotor and hub for warpage and cracks.

Lead mounting: Check that the lead pieces are on tight and cotter pinned.

Exhaust: Inspect the exhaust pipe gasket and the springs if so equipped. Most kart engines are notorious for blowing the exhaust gaskets, and the springs on two-cycles should be replaced each race or practice day.

Instrument cables: Check for kinks and burns. Check the connection. Keep the tachometer wire away from other cables, especially the spark plug high-tension lead.

Check the instruments for proper operation. The usual suspects include the battery and the leads. Sometimes the leads can look new and yet they may not work or show intermittent problems. At the first sign of trouble, replace the battery, and then try new leads.

Safety wiring or cotter pinning of bolts only prevents them from falling off. These devices do not prevent the fasteners from loosening. Safety wire after the fastener has been tightened so you will know the nut is tight.

Reed valves should be checked after each race, and replaced at the first sign of wear. These reeds are off a US820.

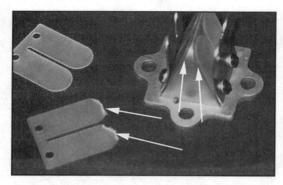

Miscellaneous: Check spark plug boot and cable, transponder battery, kill switch, all fasteners, etc.

Starter Batteries

Starter batteries should be charged immediately after use and stored in a cool environment. If the battery is to be stored for a few months, it is advisable to recharge it every thirty to sixty days or to keep a maintenance charger connected to the unit. Remember that chargers are not maintenance devices (also known as "trickle chargers") and trickle chargers are not designed to recharge a battery after it has been used.

Charge the battery immediately after each race. The amp meter on the charger indicates the rate at which the battery is charging; when the gauge reads zero, the battery is charged. Maintain it between races if the voltage drops by more than .1 volt. The deeper the battery is discharged and/or the longer it has been left discharged, the longer it will take to recharge.

Clutch Maintenance

Remove the clutch and inspect it every two races, or if the unit is used under harsh conditions (small clutch, high power, high weight or combinations of the three) inspect it after each race or practice day. Chapter 8 of this book covers clutch maintenance. Most clutch failures are caused by lack of care, infrequent inspections or over-slippage. Playing around on a parking lot with a race kart is a sure way of damaging a racing clutch. There are clutches built for "fun-karts" that can take this abuse.

The axle bearings require special attention. Check that they are tight, they run free and that the axle does not show any signs of movement. For new karters sealed bearings are a better choice over the open type.

The two major causes of battery failure include over-charging and storing when partly or fully discharged. To make the task of charging the battery easier and safer, choose a charger adequate to the task. The voltage output of the charger should not exceed 14.3 volts at 50 degrees Fahrenheit and at higher temperatures, the voltage must be lower; at 100 degrees, for example the end of charge voltage should not exceed 13.7. Check the end of charge voltage when the charger is connected to a fully charged battery. If the battery boils over when it is being recharged, it is being overcharged, or the voltage output of the charger is too high.

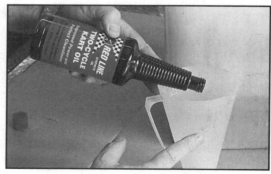

For two-cycle racing, use a Ratio-Rite to mix the oil in the fuel. These are graduated in gallons of fuel and ratio of oil you desire to run. Just pour the oil to the line and dump it in the fuel.

Helmets, Goggles and Face Shields

The first rule with maintaining a helmet is to have the manufacturer inspect it if the driver has been involved in a severe crash, particularly if there are marks on the helmet, or if the helmet has been dropped. The shell of a helmet is quite thin at about 1/16th-inch. Helmets are designed to crack like an eggshell to absorb the shock and protect the head. If the shell is already cracked or scratches or dents have weakened it, it will not serve its purpose as well as it should. Helmet shells can also weaken from sanding, or from using the wrong chemicals to remove paint or decals.

When removing the helmet after coming off the track, set it upside-down in the sun. This will allow the sun to quickly dry the sweat and kill odor causing bacteria and mold. Do not pack a sweaty helmet. Always store your helmet in a bag especially if you own pets or have small children; helmets make fun toys for kids and dogs. Store helmets in cool, dry areas and not in the garage where mice and bugs can find a home in the same space where you will be breathing for several hours next weekend. Helmets are too expensive and valuable to have them end up as a rat's nest. In such an instance, return the helmet to the manufacturer and have it relined...and deodorized.

Occasionally inspect the lining, in particular the spongy foam at the top of the helmet. This seems to be the first part of helmets to deteriorate. Look for cracks, scratches and dents. Never lend your helmet or let others handle it; this way you will know its history. Should someone else drop it and not tell you, you could be wearing an unsafe helmet. Do not play "catch" with a helmet.

Replace the face shield and the lens on your goggles often. These are inexpensive and they can prevent a lot of frustration if they are kept in good working order. (Not to mention the fact that a clear vision is a safety factor, and can be worth a few tenths on the track.) Discard lenses or shields with cracks as they can break and cause injuries. Never use a dry rag on Plexiglas, as the dust will scratch its surface. Use Plexiglas cleaner to clean face shields; this material is available at most auto-parts stores and better kart shops.

Record Keeping

Keeping records can also be helpful in tracking your expenses, some of which may be tax deductible. Phone numbers such as for hotels, suppliers, credit card companies

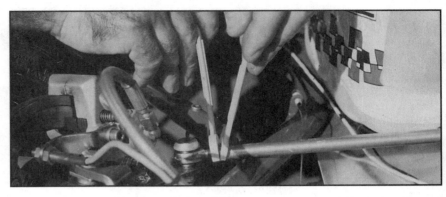

Use the correct tools especially on fragile parts like the tie rods. Allow enough movement in the rod ends when the steering is turned.

and clubs can also be recorded and kept in a separate address book. The numbers for your roadside service like the Auto Club, or your car's towing service have a place in this address book. Prescription numbers and phone number of your doctor, insurance company and pharmacist would be a good addition if you or anyone in your party is under a doctor's care. If you suffer from allergies or a chronic disease, wear an emergency bracelet. For the first outing, a record sheet will be invaluable to note the things you forgot, did not think of bringing, or simply assumed you did not need, like ice and drinks.

Maintenance Check List

- Charge starter battery as soon as possible after use.
- Helmet care and storage.
- Clean suit, neck collar and gloves.
- Run gasoline through the engine after you race on methanol.
- Gauge: battery, cables not kinked and away from spark plug wire, function.
- Drain fuel.
- Bleed brakes.
- Check brake operation and condition.
- Check compression.
- Replace tires if needed.
- Inflate and measure tires.

On Briggs with the stock carburetor, allow plenty of room between the air filter and the throttle lever (finger). Also check throttle clamp (arrow).

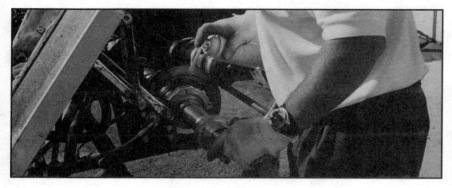

The brakes and rear axle can be cleaned with carburetor spray cleaner. It will leave the anodized and chromed parts looking "real purdy." Cover radiators when working on a shifter; it may save some grief in the future.

- Wipe off excess oil, install chain and spray lube.
- Plug gap and lube (prepare some spares?).

Use a tire-breaking tool to loosen the bead from the rim. Adjust the arms of the tool to the size of the rim.

- Check front-end toe and note (air up the tires).
- Scale the chassis (not necessary each race for beginners).
- Inspect the axle bearings and brake rotor and gear hub.
- Throttle cable and clamps.
- Clean air filter once a year (K&N filters).
- Gears: installation and alignment.
- Look for cracks in the chassis, steering and spindles.
- Check front end, spindles, tie rods, tie rod ends, steering shaft, steering wheel and its hub.
- Spin axle and listen for noisy bearings.
- Check and lube rear bearings if possible.

Use motorcycle tire dismounting tools to remove the tire. After installing the tire tool, press down on the tire at the opposite side of the wheel to introduce the bead you are trying to dismount to the hollow of the wheel.

The compression can be checked with the engine in the chassis. Ground the plug to prevent damage to the ignition. The type of gauge that screws into the spark plug hole makes things easier. Hold the throttle wide open and keep notes of the compression readings.

- Remove axle if necessary and rebuild it.
- Inspect belly pan.
- Check ballast mounting.
- Check all cotter pins required by the rules.
- Check the brake caliper bolts.
- Remove chain.
- Inspect chain and check for bent or stiff links.
- Clean the chain and bearings if they were removed from the axle.
- Place chain in a can of oil and turn it over occasionally.

Install the inside of the rim (side opposite the valve stem) into the tire. Rub a piece of soap on the outside of the rim lip. Introduce the wheel at an angle to the tire and push it in. Harder compound tires will be easier to install if left in the sun for a few minutes.

Last, slip the outside of the tire over the rim. Do not over inflate the tires to set the bead on the rim.

Chapter 13
SHIFTERS
Respect! Patience, Training

Much of the maintenance and repair procedures covered in the remainder of this text also apply to the shifters. However, with shifter karts some procedures and settings differ sufficiently to warrant a dedicated chapter. Some details are purely generic to the shifters: the engines and gearboxes, size of chain, dual brakes, water cooling system, instrumentation, shifter mechanism, the size of the wheels and the chassis themselves which differ mainly because of their front brakes, tubing size, and the mounts for the shifting mechanisms. Starting the engine also requires some practice and training.

Most adults in shifter karting run the 80 or the 125cc engines. The 60cc engines are used primarily by younger drivers. The 60 and 80cc shifters come without front brakes which makes the chassis useable in other classes of sprint karting. The Big Bad Boys of karting, the 250cc karts, are only raced by experienced and well financed drivers. These are not for every beginner.

Age Limitations
There is no set limit to decide at what age a child can start racing a kart with a gearbox, but it is recommended, however, that the child have considerable experience in a

This Vortex shifter engine is the latest entry in the race for power in North American karting. This engine and its gearbox are built specifically for karting. Note the air-cooled clutch.

Shifter Kart Illustrated is the "official" magazine of shifter karting. The magazine covers all the major events, it conducts tests and it publishes technical articles. Rob Howden is the publisher.

clutch kart before jumping in a shifter, even a restricted one. The speed can be overwhelming and even scary. If a youngster is afraid of the kart, no amount of coaxing will make him want to race. Learning how to shift a kart can be quite challenging especially to someone who may not even know which is the gas pedal and which is the brake. Knowing how to shift can be learned later when the driver is old enough to drive a passenger car. At an early age, the driver needs to concentrate on the basics of race driving techniques.

It is advisable to older drivers to be in good shape and to have a check-up from their doctor before deciding to drive a shifter. The high G loads generated by the engine and the turning can stress the muscles (primarily the neck), to the point where a driver can run out of breath and reach critical heart rate.

Engines
Lubrication

All the shifters use two-cycle engines. Follow the fuel mixing procedures as outlined in the engine chapter. Do not be concerned with loss of power and rich oil mixtures. Also, do not fall prey to 100:1 ratios some oil manufacturers claim. A 20 or 25:1 mix of real synthetic two-stroke oil like Red Line's will protect the engine and will actually increase power. The loss of power created

The shifter engines have their transmission oil filler plug at the top of the crankcase. The manufacturers have cast the amount of oil the crankcase required just below the plug. The water pump is located below the filler plug.

by the excess oil is surpassed by the power gained from the reduction in friction supplied by the oil. The oil also replaces some of the fuel, but this is compensated with the jetting.

Gearbox

Shifter karts are equipped with a gearbox and generally a wet clutch. The crankcase must be filled with the appropriate lubricant. Consult the owner's manual for your particular engine, or use a true synthetic lubricant. The gear oil should be replaced after each race; certainly if you have just purchased the kart the level should at least be checked. The gear oil should be compatible with the clutch as the linings also run in the lubricant. Do not use automatic transmission fluid in the gearbox. ATF does not contain the additive package real gear oil possesses and it is of low viscosity.

Lubricants

Unfortunately in karting there are still some "back-yard operations" which bottle oils with bases from peanut, or other cheap vegetable oils and their additive package (if any) consists of those sold in auto parts stores. The laws governing the wording for labeling of synthetic oils are not well established. Some manufacturers use the term "synthetic", but they may use a large percentage of mineral oil or castor and get away with it. Just reading the word "synthetic" or "racing" on the container does not ensure optimum quality and even synthetics come in several grades. The best synthetic oils are 100% polyol ester base-stocks, with the proper additives, in the correct balance for

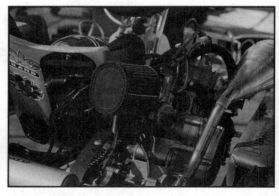

Use caution when getting in and out of the seat not to push on the air filter or the exhaust pipe. Keep the ignition and the coil as far away from each other. Honda recommends 12 to 16 inches minimum. Note the chain guard on this shifter.

the application. As with all other racing parts and components, use purpose made lubricants. A shifter kart has far different needs than a jet ski or snowmobile!

Fuel System

To most novices the fuel system causes more confusion than any other part of a shifter (outside of getting used to shifting without stepping on the brake pedal). The problem stems from the fact that with a motorcycle, the carburetor is gravity fed from the tank. On a kart, the tank is below the carburetor; without a pump, the carburetor will not receive any fuel. With a pump, the carburetor will run very rich or even flood, as the system is not designed to be pressurized. There are two methods of running the fuel system on a shifter, both include the use of a pump and some form of by-pass.

Fuel Pumps and By-pass

One of the set-ups is to use a T-fitting fed from a low pressure pump. The inlet side of the "T" comes from the outlet of the pump, one of the branches goes to the carburetor and the other returns to the tank. The branch that runs to the carburetor should run downhill, while the return line to the tank should be uphill. In this fashion, the line going to the carburetor will always be full without being pressurized and the uphill line will return the fuel not used by the carburetor to the tank. The return line should be the same size or larger than the other two. Some manufacturers offer small cans with a return hose to the tank. These units also work well. The second method is to use a fuel pump with a return hose. These pumps only pump enough fuel to keep the lines full without pressurizing the system.

Carburetors

While all three of the Japanese manufacturers use the same type of carburetors, their tuning varies considerably from engine to engine and from manufacturer to manufacturer. To some new karters tuning the carburetors is the most frustrating operation on a shifter kart. If the fuel system is not plumbed properly, it may leak and flood the engine from the excessive pressure. If not jetted correctly the engine will run poorly and make for a bad-hair day. First, install the correct fuel pump, or use a "T" fit-

ting to return the excess fuel to the gas tank. Check the float level and then follow the charts in this chapter or ask your engine builder what jets to run. Some shops specialize in shifter engines and can be of great help.

Keep in mind that these shops have spent considerable time and resources to find the optimum in carburetor tuning and they are reluctant to give out their hard-earned knowledge to their competitors' customers. The best approach is to take your carburetor and fuel pump to the shop and explain the problems you are having (or want to keep from having). The beginner who should be concerned with learning how to drive and the basics of tuning and chassis set-ups, should also ask for basic tuning parameters after he has had the carburetor rebuilt or modified.

Fuel pump and filter on a Honda shifter kart. Note the hose to return the fuel to the tank to prevent pressurising the carburetor. Choose the right pump (arrow) and fuel system or the carburetor will not operate properly.

A simple "T" fitting can solve many headaches. The fuel comes from the pump in one branch and returns to the tank in another. The third line feeds the carburetor without pressurizing it. Arrow points to ground strap.

Needle (1) and clip (2). The higher the clip is positioned, the lower the needle will sink into the jet and the leaner the engine will operate. The lower the clip is positioned on the needle the higher the needle will rest in the jet and the richer the engine will operate. Courtesy Honda.

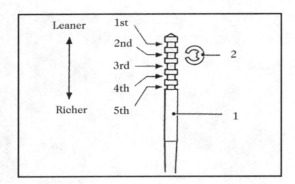

Basic Operation

Shifter carbs control the engine speed by controlling the amount of air the engine is allowed to ingest via a slide (throttle valve) controlled by the driver. The fuel is regulated by a jet orifice inside of which a tapered needle is introduced. The needle, being attached to the slide, controls the amount of fuel that passes between the needle and the jet. The higher the slide is opened, the thinner the section of the needle becomes where it enters the jet, and the larger the amount of fuel will be allowed to pass. At lower engine speeds and partial throttle openings the fuel is controlled by a low speed jet and its air compensating screw, and by the straight section of the needle which occupies approximately half of the length of the fuel metering portion of the needle. From about 1/4 to 1/2 throttle, up to full throttle the fuel is regulated by the needle and the jet. The racer should be concerned primarily with the main jet. When the engine has been modified and/or when a racing exhaust has been installed, he may also work with the needle. The feeding of the carburetor should be examined before attempting to tune the carburetor. From one extreme to another the jet size should not

exceed five to six sizes, any variation from this data indicates a problem which requires troubleshooting. If the tuner finds he needs to change the jet size by more than five or six steps, he should troubleshoot the carburetor, the pump and the fuel supply method.

The Jet, Air Screw and Needle

The main jet affects fuel mixture at full throttle. Its size will have the greatest effect on tuning. The main jet should be changed first when racing at different altitudes. Use jets from the same manufacturer as your engine, since the numbering system from one manufacturer to another varies.

The jet and needle control the fuel/air mixture from 1/4 to 1/2 throttle. The straight section affects throttle response at smaller throttle openings. The fuel mixture can be adjusted at medium low and medium speeds by changing the position of the retaining clip on the needles.

The slow jet and air screw control the air/fuel mixture at idle and very low speeds. The screw is turned to get maximum performance and the jet is only replaced when the engine has been modified. This adjustment also affects throttle response when the driver gets back on the gas when exiting a turn.

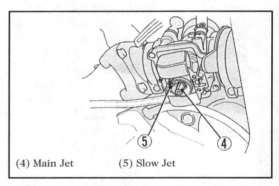

(4) Main Jet   (5) Slow Jet

To access the main and slow jets remove the carburetor bowl. The float can also be adjusted with the float bowl removed. Courtesy Honda.

The Needle Valve and Float Level

The needle valve must be checked when pulling maintenance. This valve consists of two parts: a plunger which controls the flow of fuel into the float bowl and a spring activated push-rod. Check the tapered surface of the plunger. If any marks appear, replace it immediately. Next, push the rod in the needle valve, then release it. If it does not

Diagram shows the major parts of a slide carburetor. Drawing courtesy Honda Motors.

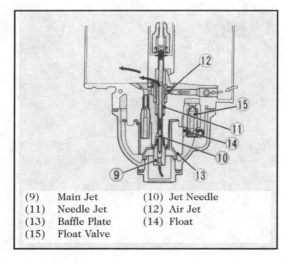

(9)	Main Jet	(10)	Jet Needle
(11)	Needle Jet	(12)	Air Jet
(13)	Baffle Plate	(14)	Float
(15)	Float Valve		

come out fully by spring tension, replace the whole needle, and check and reset the float level if necessary.

The level of the fuel in the bowl has a serious effect on the operation of the carburetor and performance of the engine. The fuel float level must be checked and reset if it is not adjusted properly. The float adjustment controls the level of the fuel in the bowl; the level influences the air/fuel mixture.

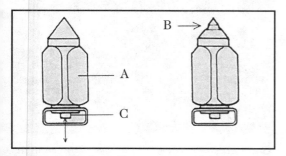

This drawing from the Kawasaki catalog shows a typical carburetor needle valve (A). Inspect the needle valve tip for wear, marks, and scratches (B). The plunger (C) should push in and return freely. Replace the whole plunger if it sticks. Courtesy Kawasaki.

At his first practice, the novice can use the stock needles and jets that come with the engines. The two carburetor parts that influence operation the most and should be closely monitored are the main jet and the needle. If the engine has been modified for karting, use a richer (larger diameter) main jet or follow the recommendations of the engine builder. Air density (air pressure and humidity), the modifications performed to the engine, (primarily the compression ratio and port enlargement), and the type of exhaust pipe used dictate the size of the main jet and needle and the position of its clip, (determines how much the needle obstructs the jet). If you race regularly at the same track find a jet that works well and stick to it unless the air density changes drastically. Run a larger main jet the closer to sea level you race and use a smaller jet at higher elevations.

Fuel

Run 105 RON octane racing fuel, especially if the compression has been increased and if you race at low elevations and in hot weather. Do not use octane boosters, aviation gas or pump gas. Use a good racing gasoline like ELF, CRC, Sunoco, Trick, Unocal, or VP. With fuel as well as oils always

rely on the established, professional companies who do testing with professional teams and who employ engineers to truly design products. Look for companies that have qualified people to answer your questions.

Spark Plugs

Shifter karts prefer resistor plugs and resistor caps. The resistor caps should be replaced every two or three races and the spark plugs should be renewed each race. Gap the plugs, no matter what the guy at the parts house tells you. Spark plugs may be "pre-gapped" at the factory but they may have been gapped for another engine, not yours. Furthermore, the gap may have been banged around in shipping or in your tool box.

Recommended spark plugs and gaps for various shifter engines:

Honda 125 = NGK BR9EG or BR10EG
    Gap .020 – .024-inch
Honda 80 = NGK BR10EG
    Gap .020 – .024-inch

Kawasaki 125 = NGK BR9EG or
    BR10EG Gap .024–.027-inch
    R6254K105 or R6385-10
    Gap .024 – .027-inch
Kawasaki 80 = R6254K105
    Gap .020-.024-inch
Kawasaki 60 = NGK B9EG or B9EVX
    Gap .020 – .024-inch

Yamaha 125 = NGK BR9EG
    Gap .020–.024-inch
Yamaha 80 = NGK BR10EG
    Gap .020 – .024-inch

Reading the Spark Plug

To read a spark plug for proper jetting look at the electrode and the interior of the plug body (on the inside of the threads).

With a properly tuned carburetor and correct heat range the ceramic will be tan in color and the electrode and interior of the threads will be gray. The leaner the mixture is and the hotter the range is the whiter the ceramic will become. The richer the carburetion, or colder the spark is, the blacker it will turn. The color of the ceramic is indicative of the heat range of the spark plug while the base of the ceramic and the interior of the spark plug indicate the mixture setting. Do not attempt to tune the carburetor until you have found the correct heat range spark plug.

Exhaust Systems

The compression, port timing and the exhaust system on a shifter have a great effect on the tuning of the carburetor. Exhaust systems increase power typically at higher engine speeds. The increase in power will require a larger amount of fuel. How much and when in the power band the fuel is needed is dictated in great part by the pipe. Consult the exhaust system builder before tuning the carburetor, or better yet have him set-up the carburetor and pump.

As a beginner, do not play the "pipe of the month" game. Find a good pipe and stick to it. A "good pipe" is not one that necessarily makes the most power, but one that is tuned to your engine and your experience. Some manufacturers, like RLV, have done extensive research on the subject and can best advise you on your particular racing needs and the tuning requirements of their systems as they relate to the carburetor. Use caution, as some pipes require a much richer mixture and their use could cause the piston to seize if the carburetor is not tuned properly.

The crankcase drain plug is easily accessible from the bottom of the engine. Replace the washer each time it is removed.

Avoid messy and power robbing exhaust leaks by replacing the exhaust gasket on a regular basis. An exhaust leak can also cause the engine to seize. Keep spares and some RTV silicone and fresh springs if you use them. The exhaust springs should be replaced after each race.

Cooling systems

The cooling system should be drained a few times each year and flushed with fresh water. Replace the coolant with straight water, or if available with distilled water. Do not use antifreeze unless the engine is to be stored or transported in freezing weather. Under normal circumstances keeping the engine from freezing is probably your last concern; keeping it cool on the track is far more important.

While antifreeze prevents the water from freezing it also makes the water much thicker and difficult to flow. Furthermore, the thicker mixture does not penetrate the small cavities of the castings and the water picks up less heat from the engine. The process is reversed in the radiator where

Cover the radiator with some heavy wire mesh. It will provide protection from stones and rubber gumballs. Keep the screen clean.

the coolant does not dissipate as much of the heat as it could without antifreeze. Granted, antifreeze will prevent water from boiling up to a more elevated temperature, but plain water and an anti corrosive cooling agent, such as Water Wetter, will run cooler in the first place. Water Wetter contains the anti corrosive agents to protect aluminum and prevent steel from rusting and aluminum from corroding.

To be certain about the integrity of the cooling system, check it with a pressure kit. A kart shop that specializes in shifter karts should own one of these and certainly a motorcycle shop will. Check all the hoses for wear, cracks, damage, and tighten all the hose clamps. Inspect the radiator, pump, hoses and engine for signs of leaks.

White deposits are telltale marks of water leakage. In this event the water should be drained and the head gasket replaced.

This device is a water temperature-sending unit for electric water temperature gauges. Note the carburetor breather hoses below. The hoses are run in a single length from one breather to another and a small cut is made to allow the float bowl to breathe.

Radiators

Radiators should be covered when the kart is not racing. Tools, parts and small dogs can easily fall on the fins and possibly cause a leak. A thick piece of cardboard or thin plywood can be used on both sides of the unit and held on with a strap or some nylon tie straps.

Radiators should be run at 15 degrees from vertical. This allows the air to spend a little more quality time in the core and this picks-up more heat. Radiators can sometimes be reduced in size or they can be partly covered if the system is very efficient, or on a cool day.

It is a good idea to drain the radiator before storage, particularly if you live in a cold climate. Keep a stock of drain plug washers and replace them each time you drain the fluid.

Water temperature gauges can be purchased from speed shops. These Auto Meter gauges are liquid filled to absorb vibrations.

Brakes

Bleeding the brakes on a shifter is essentially the same procedure as with the other karts, but bleed one master cylinder at a time. When the front and rear brakes are bled properly, check that the balance bar is perpendicular to the chassis (parallel to the rear axle) when the brakes are applied.

This prevents binding of the push rods and provides more even braking. The balance bar acts as a lever on each master cylinder. The closer the actuation rod is to one of the master cylinders, the more pressure it will apply to that cylinder. Try to set the brakes to lock the front wheels first. This will help prevent spinouts.

While the shifter karts with four-wheel brakes are equipped with dual master cylin-

ders, keep in mind that if one of the cylinders or its accompanying calipers lose pressure containment, you will lose brakes on all four wheels. What happens is that the defective master cylinder will collapse, taking up the pedal travel. The other master cylinder in turn will only be pressurized if there is some pedal travel left.

The brake pads require some more attention on shifters as they are used consider-

Use carburetor spray cleaner to clean the brakes. Never use soap or spray lubricants near the brake rotors and pads.

The two plugs near the front must be removed to bleed the brakes or to add fluid to the master cylinders. Bleed one cylinder at a time. See the maintenance chapter in this book for the procedure.

The balance bar must be perpendicular to the chassis when the brakes are applied. This prevents the push rods from binding and makes for smoother braking. The closer rod to the lever will have the greater leverage. The black knob is used to adjust the braking balance between the front and the rear brakes.

ably more rigorously than on slower, lighter karts. Special pads are available that provide long life and which prevent fading. Inspect the pads after each outing.

Driving

Learning to drive a shifter kart is somewhat different from a regular kart or an automobile. It is actually a combination of driving a car, a motorcycle and a kart. The gear shifting controls are placed under the right hand like a car, but the left pedal activates the brakes and not the clutch. This leads many newcomers to step on the brakes each time they try to shift; rather embarrassing!

Respect! A novice will quickly learn the meaning of this word when driving a shifter kart for the first time. The power-to-weight ratio on these machines is awesome and the low gearing multiplies the torque by a large amount. Slightly too much throttle pressure in a turn and the kart will go for a stint of agricultural racing faster than you can say "tractor." Needless to say that the first order of business when originally driving a shifter kart is to use the controls, especially the throttle, most gently.

Set the brakes with slightly more front bias for your first few outings. This way if too much braking power is applied the front wheels will lock-up before the rears, preventing a possible spin.

Starting

Before starting, you need to find "neutral". The neutral is between first and second. Pull the gearshift lever up several times to engage first gear. Once in first, push gently down on the lever to slip into neutral. Pull in the clutch to release all the pressure on the discs to facilitate pushing. Have your teammate push the kart while you apply a

small amount of throttle. Do not give it full throttle or the engine will not start. Once underway, pull up on the shift lever and immediately pop the clutch. If you need to stop, like at the track entrance, pull the clutch lever and apply the brakes.

When accelerating from a dead stop, it is necessary to give a lot of gas and slip the clutch very gently. The clutch can be "dumped," but in the beginning learn how to accelerate smoothly and gently. Remember that these karts can spin out from a standing start too.

Shifting

Practice shifting at home with the engine off. To up shift release the throttle pressure and pull once on the gear lever. To downshift release the throttle pedal and push down on the gear lever. Do not step on the left pedal; it is the brake, not the clutch, and the clutch does not need to be used at all to shift up or down. After you have practiced at low speed, try tapping the gas pedal while downshifting to bring the engine up to the same speed as the kart. This is the equivalent of the heel and toe technique used on cars. The driver needs to learn to time the shifting to the track and the engine speed.

Since most novices have driven a passenger car before, they tend to have a tendency to shift too early. It is OK to do so at first. After a few outings you will learn the rhythm and pitch of the engine, and shifting at the right time will become automatic. Avoid counting the gears while on the track. Try to learn to shift based on the pitch of the engine.

Tuning

Tuning a carburetor is not as complicated as it may seem; considerable information is available. The manufacturers supply technical manuals on the subject and many shops specialize in shifter engines. Consult those sources before tuning the carburetor. However, as a word of caution, when reading the literature or when consulting the shops, remember that tuning a carburetor is highly dependent on the state of tune of the engine, its modifications and its exhaust system. The ideal approach is to consult a company that manufactures exhaust pipes and modifies carburetors. Typically, these shops conduct extensive research and development and have found the optimum parameters for the carburetor and their

Starting a shifter kart engine on the stand is not easy. Put the transmission in gear, grab a rear wheel and crank away. Wear gloves and eat your Wheaties.

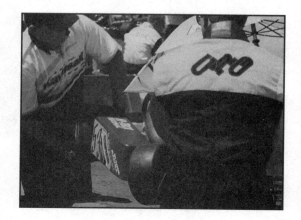

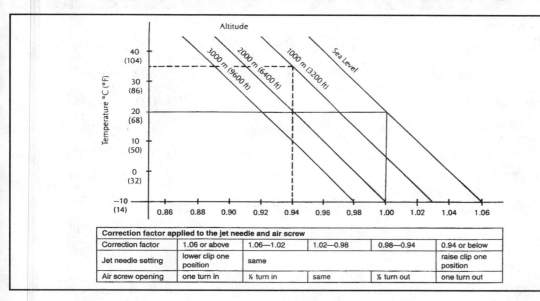

This correction factor chart will be helpful with any engine. Courtesy Honda.

Correction factor applied to the jet needle and air screw				
Correction factor	1.06 or above	1.06—1.02	1.02—0.98	0.98—0.94	0.94 or below
Jet needle setting	lower clip one position	same			raise clip one position
Air screw opening	one turn in	½ turn in	same	½ turn out	one turn out

exhausts, and they backed up their findings on the track. The information gathered from these shops is most relevant when the racer has purchased his exhaust system and had his carburetor blueprinted by them.

Air/Fuel Mixture

The air/fuel mixture requires attention if you just bought the kart, if you installed a new exhaust system, if the engine has been modified, or if you are racing at a new track of different elevation from your usual venue. Air density, altitude changes, humidity, and to a smaller extent temperature have a marked effect on the performance of an engine as it relates to the air/fuel mixture. As a rule of thumb the higher the elevation, the richer (greater amounts of fuel) the mixture should be (larger main jet, and in extreme cases or in the case of a highly modified engine, a different needle).

As the elevation increases, the air pressure decreases. As the pressure drops, the amount of oxygen in the air also diminishes. The quantity of fuel the engine uses must be calibrated to compensate for the change in the level of oxygen.

Symptoms of Improper Mixture

Too Rich a Mixture:
- Poor acceleration
- Carburetor leaks fuel
- Misfires at low speeds
- Excessive smoke
- Spark plug fouls or black color
- A deep, throaty exhaust sound

Too Lean a Mixture:
- Pinging and rattling like marbles in exhaust
- Erratic acceleration
- Feels like running out of gas
- High engine and exhaust temperatures
- Hole in the piston
- Whitish spark plug electrode and interior

Before setting the fuel mixture first check the spark plug, its wire and cap and verify the ignition timing.

Diagram shows Honda's suggested carburetor tuning based on altitude and temperature. The higher the elevation the leaner the engine should be operated. Courtesy Honda.

All jetting is based on
* Standard Jetting
* 32:1 Fuel/Oil Ratio
* Unmodified Engine (Including Porting, Exhaust and Timing)

After '98

Temperature	Cent.	−35° ~−18°	−17° ~−7°	−6° ~4°	3° ~15°	14° ~26°	25° ~38°	37° ~49°
Altitude	Fahr.	−21° ~0°	−1° ~20°	19° ~40°	39° ~60°	59° ~80°	79° ~100°	99° ~120°
3,000 m (10,000 ft)	AS:	2•1/2	2•3/4	3•1/4	3•1/2	3	3•1/4	3•1/2
	SJ:	55	55	55	55	52	52	52
	NC:	4th	4th	4th	4th	3rd	3rd	3rd
2,300 m (7,500 ft)	MJ:	182	178	175	168	165	160	155
2,299 m (7,499 ft)	AS:	2•1/4	2•1/2	2•1/4	3•1/4	3•1/2	3	3•1/4
	SJ:	55	55	55	55	55	52	52
	NC:	4th	4th	4th	4th	4th	3rd	3rd
1,500 m (5,000 ft)	MJ:	185	180	178	172	170	165	160
1,499 m (4,999 ft)	AS:	2	2•1/4	2•1/2	2•3/4	3•1/4	3•1/2	3
	SJ:	55	55	55	55	55	55	52
	NC:	4th	4th	4th	4th	4th	4th	3rd
750 m (2,500 ft)	MJ:	188	182	178	175	172	168	162
749 m (2,499 ft)	AS:	1•3/4	2	2•1/4	2•3/4	3	3•1/4	3•1/2
	SJ:	55	55	55	55	55	55	55
	NC:	5th	4th	4th	4th	4th	4th	3rd
300 m (1,000 ft)	MJ:	192	185	182	178	175	170	168
299 m (999 ft)	AS:	1•3/4	2	2•1/4	2•1/2	STANDARD 2•3/4	3	3•1/4
	SJ:	55	55	55	55	55	55	55
	NC:	5th	5th	4th	4th	JETTING 4th	4th	4th
Sea level	MJ:	192	188	185	180	178	175	170

Legend
AS: Air Screw opening from fully seated
SJ: Slow Jet
NC: Needle Clip position
MJ: Main Jet

SUPPLIERS

Adams Kart Track
Riverside CA
800 350-3826

APS
Newbury, OH
440 564-8100

Arsenal
Neptune Beach, FL
904 241-1170

Auto Books
Burbank, CA
818 845-1909

Bergfelt Racing
Beaver Falls, PA
724 847-3677

Best Racing
Willowbrook, IL
630 455-4960

Bob's Kart Shop
Sheridan, IL
815 496-2820

Bondurant School
Chandler, AZ
800 652-5278

Bones Kart Shop
Milford, CT
203 783-9925

Buller Built
Henderson, NE
402 723-4713

Cal Kart
San Jose, CA
408 293-3702

Capone Kart Shop
Redding, PA
610 478-1125

Carlson Racing
Linden, IN
765 339-4407

CKT Motorsports
Elburn, IL
630 365-6733

Comet Kart Sales
Greenfield, IN
317 462-3413

Competition Karting
Welcome, NC
336 731-6111

Dave Turner
San Diego, CA
619 571-3811

Dromo One
Orange, CA
714 744-4779

E.J.'s Creations
Aurora, OH
330 562-1651

Emmick Enterprises
Sacramento, CA
916 383-2288

Empire Karts
Redlands, CA
909 793-9695

Flat Out Group
Mundelein, OH
877 837-9200

Fox Valley Kart Shop
Lafayette, IN
765 742-0935

Franklin Motorsports
Oak Creek, WI
414 764-1884

Grand Products
Bensalem, PA
215 244-1940

Hearn Competition
Arcadia, CA
626 574-0890

High Rev Engineering
Clovis, CA
559 297-7182

Innovative Racing
Glendale, AZ
602 588-0482

JM Racing
Arcadia CA
626 446-5443

John's Kart Shop
Chicago, IL
773 586-5600

K&P MFG,
AZUSA, CA
626 334-0334

KAM Karting
Forth Worth, TX
817 589-2625

Kansas City Kart
Kansas City, MO
800 455-0654

Kart Zone
Morgan Hill, CA
408 779-7416

Kartshop.com
Brownsburg, IN
800 944-4885

L&T Manufacturing
Azusa, CA
626 334-6800

L.A.D. Specialties
Bridgeview, IL
708 430-1588

Maroon's Karts
Peoria, IL
309 637-5278

MISI
Tulsa, OK
918 835-1338

Moto World
Modesto, CA
209 527-2557

MRP
Baroda, MI
616 422-2926

Nash Muffler & Karts
Upland, CA
909 981-9611

North American
Schererville, IN
800 301-0850

O&H Kart Sales
Dallas, TX
972 243-8886

Oakland Valley
Cuddebackville, NY
914 754-8500

Pfau Distributing,
Portland, OR
503 283-1026

Pitts Performance
Van Nuys, CA
818 780-2184

Pocahontas Buggy
Madison, MS
601 366-6665

Profile Racing
Addison, IL
630 871-1964

Race Central
Portland, OR
503 283-8426

Race Kart Eng.
Paso Robles, CA
805 238-7060

Rapid Racing
Clermont, IN
317 293-2999

Rick Racing
Bow, NH
603 224-9264

Robinson Speed Shop
Pittsville, MD
410 835-2183

Russell Karting
Raymore, MO
800 821-3359

S&M Kart Supply
Springfield, IL
217 546-9120

Sheridan Racing
West Bend, WI
414 338-7745

Shift Kart
Mnt. Lake Terrace, WA
425 672-8806

T.S. Racing,
Bushnell, FL
352 793-9600

Target Distributing,
South Bend, IN
219 272-0252

Terry Ives Industries,
Citrus Heights, CA
916 725-6776

Texas Race Karts
Cypress, TX
281 256-2959

TNR Kartsport,
Canoga Park, CA
818 701-7151

Track Magic Racing
San Francisco, CA
415 822-6795

Uncle Frank's
Council Bluffs, IA
712 322-6664

Yamaha of America
Buena Park, CA
714 523-3963

CANADA
Yellow Fin, Ont.
905 525-6555

Italian Motors, B.C.
604 253-4248

S.H. Karting, P.Q.
450 584-3834

Blockzilla

It's a monster!

CRUSHING THE COST OF HIGH PERFORMANCE RACING

New Heavy Duty 5 h.p.

Briggs and Stratton Racing block

Edelbrock high performance cylinder head

Accepts stock ignition, crankshaft, and valve train

Stock deck height

Angled ports for **better flow**

Cast ribs from deck to crankcase; no stud girdle required

Cast from **356T7** for strength, machinability, and weldability

Comes with standard bore and seat sizes

Dual bearing block
Reinforced lifter bosses

Briggs and Stratton Motorsports introduces a monster of a racing cylinder/block for racers wanting BIG horsepower. Blockzilla will accept all production and high-performance Raptor-based components. This will be the only way to go for Jr. Dragsters and "open-class" kart racing. Low initial cost and ruggedness promise to bring the cost of campaigning the hottest engines to a very comfortable level.

Blockzilla Kit [555263] Includes Cylinder and Edelbrock Head • Side Cover [555216]

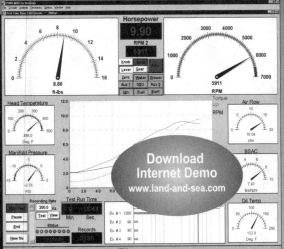
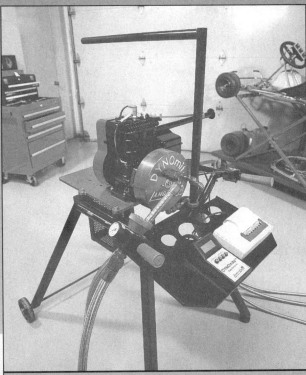

THINK FAST.
THINK AFFORDABLE.
THINK HONDA.

Winning has always been within your power. Now it's also within your price range.

Honda Engines are proving their superiority at race tracks all across the country. They're winning straight off the shelf—without costly modifications. And, best of all, they're winning on affordability too.

Honda's world-renowned engineering and technology have produced a line of highly affordable, high-performance engines that put more "go" into go karts than ever before.

In fact, the Quarter Midgets of America was so impressed, it created its own "box-stock" Honda class, which has made open wheel racing affordable for practically anyone.

So now you can blow the competition away...without blowing your budget. It all starts with a Honda. For more information please call 1-800-426-7701

www.honda-engines.com

KT100S

"THE LEADER IN KART RACING"

- Approved by all the major sanctioning bodies in the United States, Canada and Mexico.

- More National Championship titles have been won with the Yamaha KT100S.

- Over 130 dealers ready to provide support with genuine Yamaha spare parts.

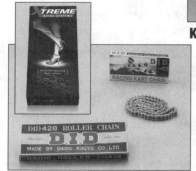

The Authority
in Shifter Kart Racing.

Speed. Excitement. Action. Stars.

And no one can bring these to you better than Shifter Kart Illustrated. As the sport's first and only magazine dedicated to gearbox racing, each issue of SKI will bring you closer to the sport with in-depth articles on the people, the equipment and the events that are shaping its future.

It's a magazine for the shifter kart enthusiast written and produced by one of the most respected journalists in the sport. So get onside and join the team. For only $23, you'll get all the inside news, serious race reports and reviews on the newest and hottest equipment available. Beginning in the Year 2000, we will be increasing our frequency to nine (9) issues a year so that we can bring you the inside information faster and more in-depth. Shifter kart racing is growing and so are we. If you like kart racing, you love the Shifter Kart Illustrated!

SUBSCRIPTION RATES - nine (9) issues
United States.........$23 (U.S. Funds)
Canada..................$30 (CDN Funds)
Foreign..................$60 (U.S. Funds)

SIMPLY SEND A CHECK OR MONEY ORDER TO:
SHIFTER KART ILLUSTRATED
1074 CHERRIEBELL ROAD
PORT CREDIT, ONTARIO
CANADA L5E 2R3

OR PRINT OUT A SUBSCRIPTION FORM
AT OUR WEBSITE:

www.shifterkartmag.com

SUBSCRIBE TODAY AND DON'T MISS A *SHIFT!*

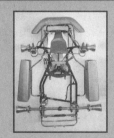

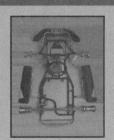

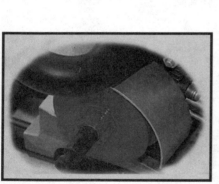